MW01629147

EADQUARTERS
BRANCH
M.C.A. EXPANSION
CAMPAIGN
TO 10th
BOYS OF DAYTON

Margaret Peters
February 25, 1996

The records of our past help us to appreciate our place in the present. The sponsors of *Dayton's African American Heritage: A Pictorial History* are proud to have a part in preserving the African American Heritage of Dayton through the presentation of this pictorial history. We hope this book will encourage interest and appreciation of African American culture, as well as recognize the significant importance of the struggles and triumphs of African Americans in Dayton over the past two hundred years. The proceeds from this volume will benefit the National Afro-American Museum and Cultural Center. The publication of this volume is made possible by the generosity of the following organizations:

DAYTON'S AFRICAN

(This Page) Linden Recreation Center at 334 Norwood began in 1906 as a playground opened by the efforts of E. T. Banks. In 1926 Captain Robert Mallory led a campaign seeking a tax levy to improve the facility. After voters approved the levy in 1928, the ground was cleared by these men so the house used as a center could be replaced by a modern building. In 1995, the center continues to serve the community. Courtesy of Linden Center.

(Cover Page) In 1926, these men gathered in front of the Stokes home on Fifth near Charter to help raise the funds to build the Fifth Street YMCA. Those identified are, first row, from the left: (5) Captain Robert Mallory, (7) Dr. Bert A. Rose, (8) James Parsons Jr., (9) J. Gilbert Waiters, and (10) Dr. Lloyd Hathcock. Second row: (1) John Green, (2) William O. Stokes, (3) Dr. Donald Gillim, (14) Reverend T. J. Smith, and (17) Dick Sloan. Third row: (9) Joe Shaw Sr., and (13) Hazey P. Loritts. On the steps at the right are Dr. Adolphus Biggs (the tall man), James Parsons Sr. (to his right), and A. W. Payne (in front of Dr. Biggs). Courtesy of Alberta Robinson Sloan.

A Pictorial History By Margaret E. Peters

AMERICAN HERITAGE

A project of the National Afro-American Museum and Cultural Center

THE DONNING COMPANY PUBLISHERS

Community organizations were an important part of the lives of black Daytonians. Around 1924, James Morris (left end) and these boys gathered at the Dayton Forum, 426 West Fifth Street, to gain support for the YMCA. The boys identified include, first row from left: (2) Joe Shaw Jr., (6) Gene Robinson, (14) Paul Hickman, (16) John Vinzant, (18) Henry Clay, and (20) Joseph Lee. Second row: (6) William Lee, (8) Obie Alcorn, and (12) Clytus Grigsby. Back row: (2) John Eaton, (4) Dick Kidd, and (12) John Carpenter. Courtesy of Joe Shaw Jr.

For information, write:

The Donning Company/Publishers
184 Business Park Drive, Suite 106
Virginia Beach, VA 23462
Steve Mull, General Manager
Debra Y. Quesnel, Project Director
Laura D. Hill, Director of Research
Dawn V. Kofroth, Production Manager
Mary Jo Kurten, Editor
Cynthia Dooley, Graphic Designer
Tony Lillis, Director of Marketing

The use of the CD'96 Logo is for promotional and educational purposes only regarding the 1996 Celebration Dayton Bicentennial

Library of Congress Cataloging-in-Publication Data

Peters, Margaret, 1936–
Dayton's African American heritage : a pictorial history / by Margaret Peters.
p. cm.
Includes bibliographical references (p.186) and index.
ISBN 0-89865-945-0 (alk. paper)
1. Afro-Americans—Ohio—Dayton—History. 2. Afro-Americans—Ohio—Dayton—History—Pictorial works. 3. Dayton (Ohio)—History. 4. Dayton (Ohio)—History—Pictorial works. I. Title.
F499.D29N47 1995
977.1'73000496073—dc20 95-369
CIP

Printed in the United States of America

Contents

The West Side Day Nursery began in 1918 when Gertrude Brown saw the need for a free nursery for working mothers. She spoke with community leader Marian Anderson, who obtained support from the Peace Chest (United Way). The nursery opened in a cottage on Fitch Street. Members of the 1920s Board of Directors included, seated from left, (3) Isabel Belboder. Standing: (1) Marian Anderson, (3) Rose Parsons, and (4) Dora Rice, Dayton's first black policewoman. In 1958 the nursery was renamed the Melissa Bess Day Care Center in honor of its long-time director. Courtesy of the Melissa Bess Day Care Center, Inc.

FOREWORD

The National Afro-American Museum and Cultural Center was chartered by the State of Ohio in 1972 and by the United States Congress in 1980 to educate the public on the history of African Americans. The Museum accomplishes this goal through a variety of means including: collecting, preserving, exhibiting, and interpreting the black experience. *Dayton's African American Heritage: A Pictorial History* is a project that satisfies all of the goals of the Museum's mission.

Out of a desire to become more involved in the Dayton and Greater Miami Valley community, the staff of the Museum organized a number of focus groups in which citizens were invited to express their opinions about the museum. Focus group participants were encouraged to list ways that the museum could be more involved in the city. The group's suggestions resulted in the Afro-American Museum's sponsorship of an exhibition and historical survey of Dayton's black community. It is hoped that the project will be a significant contribution to the legacy of the community, as well as a celebration of the bicentennial of the city's founding.

Having known Margaret Peters long before I moved to the Miami Valley, I knew that Ms. Peters, the leading authority on the history of blacks in Dayton, was the one to research and write the story. We extend our thanks for a job well done. It was fortuitous that Donning Publishers of Virginia Beach, Virginia, a well known and respected publisher of community histories, contacted me regarding this project. We soon embraced the idea and sought the support of the leading businesses in the community. We garnered the commitment of Bowman Funeral Chapel, Bob Ross Buick, Wise Construction Company, The Mead Corporation, and National City Bank to serve as financial backers of the project. To our sponsors: we are eternally indebted for your faith and trust, as well as your willingness to believe in the community's future by investing in its past. Finally, we thank the many citizens of Dayton—as individuals and members of organizations, for their support and loan of historical materials.

Dayton has a remarkable history. In many ways it has reflected the growing pains of a nation struggling with the question of what to do with its "Negro" citizens during its development. Both the new nation and the city finally accepted the role that blacks would play in their development. It has always been obvious that Dayton has a rich black cultural heritage. From the first religious congregations organized before the Civil War, to the recent rise of the Omega Baptist Church, Dayton has produced more "greats" who went on to impact the culture of the nation than any other city of comparable size. For these great accomplishments, Dayton, we salute you as a city and a community, and applaud these numerous organizations and individuals who have contributed to your greatness. The National Afro-American Museum and Cultural Center is pleased to present you this legacy for the celebration of the 200th year of your founding.

John E. Fleming, Ph.D.
Director
National Afro-American Museum and Cultural Center
Wilberforce, Ohio

PREFACE

This book was written to provide a survey of Dayton's African American community from 1798 to the present, and to look toward the twenty-first century. Previous publications have dealt with specific eras and events, but no single volume has dealt with the almost two hundred years of black history in Dayton.

The contributions of the many individuals and organizations who helped make this publication possible are deeply appreciated. The book is a project of the National Afro-American Museum and Cultural Center. The major sponsors are Bowman Funeral Chapel, National City Bank, The Mead Corporation, Bob Ross Buick, and Wise Construction Company.

The staffs of the City of Dayton, the Dayton City Schools, the *Dayton Daily News,* the Dayton and Montgomery County Public Library, the Montgomery County Historical Society, the Montgomery County Records Center and Archives, the National Afro-American Museum and Cultural Center, the Ohio Historical Society, and Wright State University's Paul Laurence Dunbar Archives were knowledgeable and helpful.

The people I had the pleasure of interviewing were eager to share photographs and memories. The works of pioneer historians Charles Austin, Robert Rice, and Luther White were invaluable.

One book cannot include all of the people and events that deserve inclusion. This book is dedicated to the memories and legacies of those who are included and those whom space would not allow us to include, as well as to those who will continue to enhance and to write about Dayton's African American heritage.

Margaret Peters
January, 1995

(Left) The Johnson family was living on Germantown Street when this photograph was taken around 1906. Mrs. Johnson is shown with Irene (left) and Juanita (right). Widowed soon after Irene's birth, Mrs. Johnson supported her family by washing and ironing the large aprons worn by employees at Rike's Department Store. Courtesy of Juanita Johnson Senior.

(Above) Harvey Howe and his wife, Esther Oldwine Howe, enjoy a day off. Harvey worked for the Talbott family as a chauffeur; Esther worked for them as a cook. Courtesy of Wanda Sloan.

(Right) Charity Davis was born free in Kentucky in 1802 and was brought to Dayton as a child by her father, John Davis. Here she met and married John Broady. Charity was a "conductor" on the Underground Railroad. According to family tradition, fugitive slaves would hide in the Broady home, slip into First Wesleyan Methodist Church which was next door, put on clothes provided by the church members, and then continue their journey to freedom. Johnson, First Wesleyan, *courtesy of Emma Johnson Smith.*

INTRODUCTION

In 1796, the first non-Native American settlers came to Dayton from Cincinnati, Ohio. While the names of the first white settlers can be found in many books about Dayton's history, the first references to black people did not include their names. In 1798, the first reference to an African American appeared in a Dayton Township tax listing: "William Maxwell and his negro." (Drury, *A History of Dayton*) The first black woman of record in Dayton itself was a "colored girl" whom community leader Daniel Cooper "brought here to be a servant to his family." (Edgar, *Pioneer Life)*

From this small beginning, the early black population of Dayton increased slowly due to local and state restrictions; however, not even these restrictions could limit the steady flow of black people into Ohio and the village of Dayton on the Miami River.

The omission of the names of the first two African Americans is not surprising. Although slavery was forbidden in Ohio under the provisions of the Northwest Ordinance, black people were not welcome; they were seen as competitors for the available jobs.

Therefore, in 1804, Ohio passed the first restrictive "Act to Regulate Black and Mulatto Persons." The act declared that black people entering Ohio had to present certificates of freedom. No white person could employ a black person unless he had a certificate of freedom. Those who violated the law were subject to a fine of from ten to fifty dollars. Anyone harboring a fugitive slave or hindering the recapture of a fugitive slave was subject to the same fine. In addition, if the "owner" of a black employee appeared, the employer also had to pay him fifty cents for each day of employment. Black people already in Ohio had to register and pay a fee of twelve and a half cents for themselves and their children. (Davis, "Nineteenth Century Blacks")

The records of Benjamin Van Cleve, clerk of courts, show that the following African Americans registered in Montgomery County between August 14, 1804, and February 18, 1805, entering their names of record: William Patterson, a free black man about forty years old; Benjamin Nixon, a free black man about twenty-two years old; Reuben Waggoner, a free black man about twenty-six years old, also registered his wife Margaret and his two sons, Elijah and Benjamin; Hannah Waggoner, Reuben's mother, a free black woman; David Hill, a free black man about twenty-six years old, also registered his wife Polly and his infant daughter, Miriam; and "Sarah Ball, a negro woman, thirty years old, (by her indenture from Andrew Wood to Colonel Patterson, assigned by said Patterson to James Brown, by him to Richard Meredith, by him to the said Sarah Ball, for the consideration therein mentioned)." (*Registers*)

In 1983, three generations of Carters showed the strength of the black family. In the back row are son Charles, grandson Eddie Allen, son William P. Carter, son James, father/musician William B. Carter, son-in-law Robert Caldwell Jr., and son Samuel. Middle: daughter Peggy Jones, daughters-in-law Ruth and Cynthia, mother/inventor/teacher Iula Carter with grandson Renard Caldwell, daughter Theresa, granddaughter Teri Lyn Dix and her mother Marva. Front: Countess Oliver, Anise Jones, Constancia Carter, James Carter Jr., Robert Caldwell III, and Tyrice Jones. Courtesy of the Carter family.

Those same records also show that before Edward and Lucy Page could register as free black people, they had to go to court to obtain their freedom from Robert Patterson. The Court of Common Pleas declared that they were "unjustly detained in slavery contrary to the laws and Constitution of the State of Ohio" and directed that they be liberated. (*Registers*)

Indentured servitude was not limited to adults like Sarah Ball. On August 30, 1805, the Overseers of the Poor bound out two-and-one-half-year-old Harry Cooper, son of the black girl in Daniel Cooper's possession, to Cooper. Harry was to faithfully obey Cooper's lawful commands, keep his secrets and behave in a becoming manner toward Cooper, his heirs or his assigns. Cooper promised to teach Harry farming, milling, and reading and writing, if Harry was capable of learning. He was also to provide boarding, lodging, and suitable clothing. When Harry became twenty-one, he was to be freed and given two suits of clothes and a second-rate horse and saddle. (*Deeds Book B*)

In August 1806, Harry's nine-month-old sister Polly was indentured to Daniel Cooper. Her indenture paper was similar to Harry's, but there were differences. The black girl (who still was not referred to by name) was now "living with" not "in the possession of" Daniel Cooper. Polly would be freed when she became eighteen. Like Harry, she would receive two suits of clothes, but instead of a second-rate horse, she would receive "a feather bed & bedding, plates, cups & saucers, knives & forks for a common table." (*Deeds Book*)

Unfortunately, a fire destroyed many of the records from this era. Thus, as historian Charles Austin wrote after fifteen years of research (*History of Black People*), many questions remain unanswered. Was Harry and Polly's father brought to Dayton? If so, why did Edgar not mention him? Was the family separated and only the "colored girl" brought here? Were other black people in Dayton also, as the Common Pleas Court had noted, "unjustly detained in slavery contrary to the laws and Constitution of Ohio"?

The records that are available and which include the stories of Harry (the first black child born in Dayton), Polly, and other early African Americans show that black people did not enjoy the freedom and opportunities many people assume they enjoyed because Ohio was a free state.

The freedom and opportunities they did have were limited by additional state legislation designed to regulate black people. Acts passed from 1807 through 1834, including "An Act to Amend the Act Entitled 'An Act to Regulate Black and Mulatto Persons,'" contained the following restrictions:

1. No black person could enter Ohio unless, within twenty days, two white freeholders would post a $500 bond guaranteeing his good behavior.
2. No black person could give evidence in a trial involving a white person.
3. No black person could serve on a jury.
4. Black children were denied admission to the state common school system.
5. Blacks were barred from serving in the militia.

(Davis, "Nineteenth Century Blacks")

These legislative acts formed the Ohio Black Laws, designed to be so restrictive that blacks were not only discouraged from migrating to Ohio, but were also "encouraged" to leave the state. However, there were a number of mitigating circumstances in nineteenth century Ohio which facilitated black migration into Dayton. For many blacks seeking to flee slavery and escape to Canada, Ohio often was the shortest route to freedom. There were a number of individuals and groups who actively participated in the Underground Railroad. In Ripley, "conductors" included John Parker and John Ripley, while in Dayton they included Charity Broady, Luther Bruen, Dr. Hibbard Jewett, and Joe and Nettie Piner. The house at 3525 Dandridge allegedly served as an Underground Railroad station.

In addition, abolitionists were very active in Ohio from Cincinnati to Oberlin. In spite of the hardships imposed by the Ohio Black Laws, slavery was prohibited.

All of these factors contributed to a modest increase in the black population of Dayton. By 1820, the census reported 141 free persons of color.

The photographs and written material in the following chapters will show how these early African Americans and those who came later overcame many obstacles and created Dayton's rich African American heritage. The chapters reveal participation in the arts, community/social organizations, education, family life, national events, politics and the struggle for human rights, religious life, sports, and entertainment, and the world of work.

The material in Chapters One through Four is arranged chronologically and details activities from 1798 through 1960. Chapter Five showcases Fifth Street as the center of black life from the 1920s through the 1950s, and highlights Dayton's role as a mecca for black music, producing and attracting great performers. Chapter Six summarizes the period from the 1960s through 1994, and looks forward to the twenty-first century.

Paul Laurence Dunbar, an important part of Dayton's African American heritage, wrote that "Each year has seen you, my brothers, progress." (Luckey, *Dunbar and Dayton*) As Dayton's bicentennial approaches, may this book provide the inspiration that will help us continue to progress and to build upon the heritage bequeathed to us.

This is the Miami-Erie Canal as it appeared to those standing on East Third and looking north along what is now Patterson Boulevard. Black men—many of whom lived in "Africa," the black settlement along Seely's Basin in East Dayton—helped build the canal. Excavation began at the basin between Second and Third in 1827. The canal reached Piqua in 1837 and Lake Erie in 1845, and greatly enhanced Dayton's economy. Courtesy of the Dayton and Montgomery County Pubic Library.

CHAPTER ONE

1820 – 1875

In 1820 the woods at the edge of Dayton—a town with 1,139 residents—were at Third and Charter. However, by 1875 Dayton had emerged as a city with a total population of 30,473. The African American population grew slowly, increasing from 141 to 548 during this period. *(U.S. Census)*

These Daytonians had to deal with both day-to-day problems and the problems arising from the issue that was troubling the entire country—the existence of slavery in a country that spoke of equality and God-given inalienable rights.

The story of how Dayton's black residents dealt with these problems is the subject of this chapter in the creation of Dayton's African American heritage.

In 1830 Catherine Sells married Joseph Wheeler, who was born in Virginia in 1795. Emancipated by his owner in 1805, he later worked his way to Highland County, Ohio, and was reunited with his mother, Rose, in 1814. He came to Dayton in 1824. The family he and Catherine began has played a significant role in Dayton's history in the areas of law enforcement, the preservation of local black history, music, and community/fraternal organizations. Wheeler, History of Wesleyan, *courtesy of Josephine J. Wheeler Robinson.*

In 1842, members of First Wesleyan Methodist Church built this church on Short Wilkinson Street near Bruen and Ziegler. After growing abolitionist power led to the repeal of the Black Laws in 1849, Wesleyan's basement became Dayton's first public school for black children. In 1854, a new brick building was erected on the same site to house the growing congregation. In 1915, the congregation moved to a new building at Scott and Bruen. In 1965, the congregation moved to its present location at 401 Gramont. Johnson, First Wesleyan.

Oh, Freedom

Like those who worked on the canal, Thomas Mitchell sought opportunity in Dayton, but in 1832 he was arrested, taken before a justice, and accused of being the slave of Kentuckian J. W. Deinkard. Dissatisfied with the evidence, the justice discharged Thomas. A few weeks later, armed men seized Thomas on Main Street and tried to take him away. Angry Daytonians stopped them. The men went to the justice with new evidence, and the judge declared that Thomas belonged to Deinkard.

Antislavery Daytonians offered to buy his freedom, and money was subscribed, including fifty dollars from Thomas. The owner refused the offer and came to take Thomas back to Kentucky. On January 22 the group reached Cincinnati and stopped at the Main Street Hotel. Thomas was put in a guarded room on the fourth floor. At about one o'clock, moved by

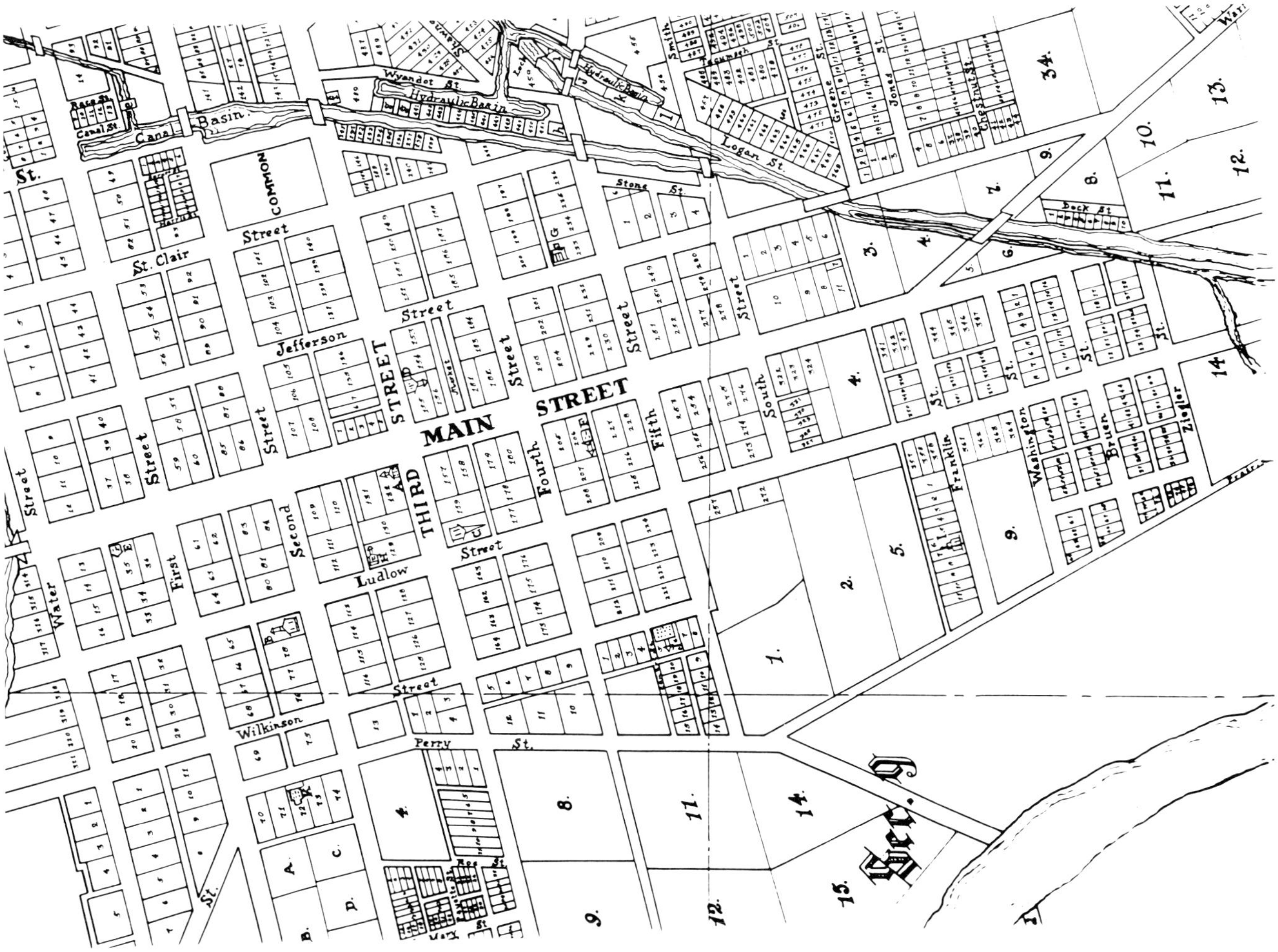

This 1839 map shows the canal, the canal basin where "Africa" was located, Main Street where Thomas Mitchell was captured, and the East Dayton area (Washington, Bruen, Ziegler, and Franklin) where Wayman Chapel AME and First Wesleyan Methodist Churches were established. After West Dayton (Miami City) was platted in 1845, the population began to move west. A pattern of black migration and white retreat that would be repeated in Edgemont, the Summit Street area, Westwood, Residence Park, and Dayton View began to develop. (Rice, "Blacks in Dayton") Courtesy of the Engineering Department, City of Dayton.

On November 30, 1870, Zion (Third) Baptist Church, Dayton's oldest black Baptist church, was organized in the Moody home on Mound Street in Miami City. After meeting in various homes and halls, the congregation erected this building at 40 Sprague Street in 1876. In 1906 black contractors William Lucius Avery and William Daugherty built a new edifice. The extension of Edwin Moses Boulevard made relocation necessary, and in 1984 the congregation moved to 1684 Earlham. Zion is the mother church of Bethel, Mt. Pisgah, Mt. Olive, and Corinthian. Drawing by Kerry Andrew Brame.

African Americans in Dayton recognized the need to form organizations. Joseph J. Wheeler was a member of the American Sons of Protection, a mutual aid society formed in 1849 because black Daytonians were denied benefits from money collected as taxes. The society prospered and helped the black community. It aided victims of the 1913 flood and owned several thousand dollars worth of property by 1916. Courtesy of Josephine J. Wheeler Robinson.

"even the faint prospect of escape or perhaps predetermined on liberty or death, [Thomas] threw himself from the window which is upwards of fifty feet from the pavement." (Steele, *History*) Thomas died, and Deinkard took his body to Kentucky for burial in his own churchyard.

Thomas was a hard-working, thoughtful man. Before he was taken away, he gave his wife and child the money he had saved.

Thomas's death intensified antislavery feelings in Dayton.

William and George W. Wheeler were the Junior Deacon and the Treasurer, respectively, of Ancient Square Lodge No. 40, organized on July 4, 1871. The other officers of this Prince Hall Masonic organization were Lot Dower, Worshipful Master; Isaac Williams, Senior Warden; Preston Findley, Junior Warden; Solomon Day, Secretary; John Butler, Senior Deacon; and Jerome Cowan, Tyler. Other organizations formed during this period included the United Daughters of Zion, the Lincoln Guards, Peters' Glee Club, and Wheeler's Brass Band. Courtesy of Josephine J. Wheeler Robinson.

Faith in God helped sustain black Daytonians. Wayman Chapel African Methodist Episcopal (AME) Church, Dayton's oldest black church, traces its origin to a listing in the minutes of the 1833 Ohio AME Conference. In 1840, this building at Plum and McLain was dedicated. In 1923 the congregation moved from a building on Eaker Street near Franklin to a new building at Fifth and Bank Streets, where it remained until the construction of the freeway forced it to relocate. The members now worship at 3317 Hoover. Courtesy of the Dayton and Montgomery County Public Library.

On December 31, 1862, Daytonians gathered at First Wesleyan Methodist Church. They and others throughout the country were waiting to see if the preliminary Emancipation Proclamation issued on September 22 would go into effect. At midnight they learned it had, and the meeting ended with shouts and tears of joy. (Johnson, First Wesleyan*) The proclamation changed the Civil War into a war for freedom. After black men were allowed to join the Union forces, 185,000 served as soldiers. William Hunter, a member of the 127th Ohio Volunteer Infantry, was one of the forty-six black Daytonians who served. Drawing by Kerry Andrew Brame.*

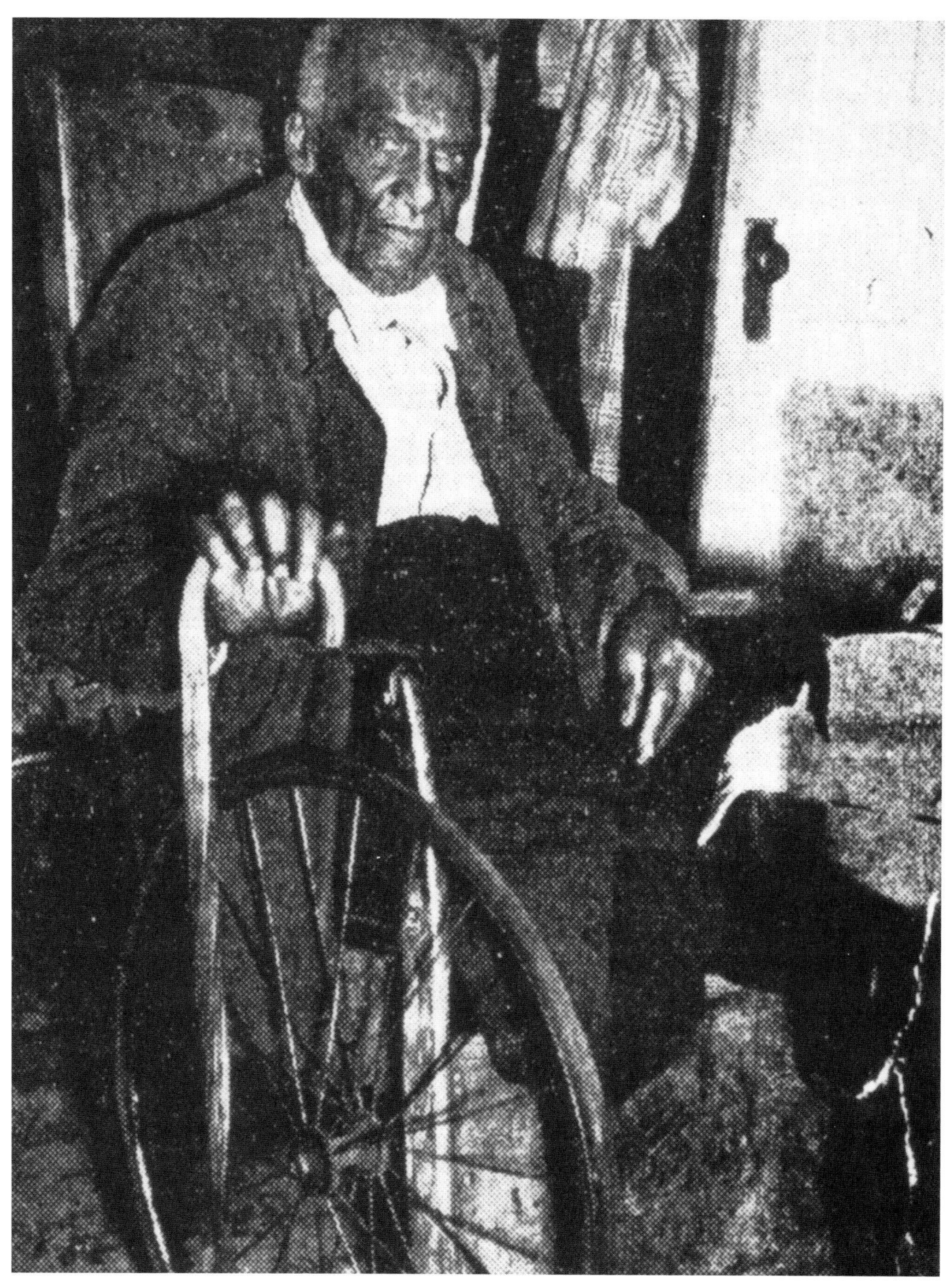

David Moody, seen celebrating his one hundredth birthday in 1938, enlisted in the army in Xenia in 1863. A member of the Twenty-seventh U. S. Volunteer Infantry, Moody fought in nine major battles, including Gettysburg. He came to Dayton after the war. Kentucky-born Jordan Schooler also came to Dayton after the war. Schooler served in Company C, 124th Colored Infantry. Courtesy of the Dayton Daily News.

Matilda Murphy, who had been a slave in Kentucky, also came to Dayton after the war with her sons, William and Robert. Here she met Joshua Dunbar. Joshua had escaped from slavery to freedom in Canada, but had chosen to return and serve in the Fifty-fifth Massachusetts Infantry Regiment. Matilda and Joshua wed, and on June 27, 1872, their son was born. Joshua named him Paul because, like Paul of the New Testament, he would be a great man. Joshua worked as a hatmaker and a whitewasher, and Matilda took in washing. Johnson, First Wesleyan.

The World Of Work

1820 — 1875

From 1820 to 1875, black Daytonians worked in many occupations. Some owned businesses. In 1820 John Crowder and Jacob Musgrave began taking passengers to and from Cincinnati in their coach, pulled by four horses. In 1871 Harriet Boone opened her first beauty salon at Second and Main. However, as this period ended, most black Daytonians were in labor/service jobs. Census data show that the top five jobs were private servants, laborers, public servants, washer women, and hostlers. Like Matilda and Joshua Dunbar, these men and women had dignity and dreams for their children.

In 1870, after Colored First Voters was formed, the Board of Education turned an old building on Ziegler and Ludlow into the new "colored" school. In 1875 black parents in Miami City petitioned the board for a school in their own neighborhood. The board granted the petition. Space in an old firehouse at Fifth and Baxter (Dunbar) became the new school, and Hallie Q. Brown (right with nieces Frances and Lois Brown) was appointed as teacher. Black Daytonians had united and had achieved a common goal. From the Frances E. Hughes Collection, courtesy of the National Afro-American Museum and Cultural Center.

After the death of Joshua Dunbar, who is buried in the National Cemetery in Dayton, Matilda and Paul struggled to support themselves. She took in laundry, which he delivered. She shared stories about her experiences, and encouraged Dunbar to write and to continue his education. In 1891 Dunbar graduated magna cum laude *from Central High School at Fourth and Wilkinson. The previous year he had published the* Dayton Tattler, *Dayton's first black newspaper. The printing was done by Orville (center, rear) and Wilbur Wright, whose printing business was at the southeast corner of Third and Williams. The Wright-Dunbar National Aviation Heritage Park honors the friendship and the legacies of these Daytonians. Courtesy of the Montgomery County Historical Society.*

Chapter Two

1876 – 1920

As the United States celebrated its centennial, black Daytonians continued to struggle to educate their children, to work at various occupations, and to found churches and other organizations. The first licensed black doctor (William Burns, Dunbar's close friend) and the first licensed black dentist (Warner A. Jackson) opened their offices before the turn of the century.

In the first decade of the new century, Moses Moore opened Dahomey (Dehoma) Amusement Park at Lakeview and Germantown. In the second decade, the flood and World War I produced stories of compassion and heroism. The Dayton branch of the NAACP was formally organized at Zion Baptist Church with J. C. Farrow, president; Moses Jones, vice president; William O. Stokes, secretary; Louise Troy, treasurer; and Reverend R. T. James, chaplain.

By 1920, the 9,052 black Daytonians represented a ten-fold increase over the 1890 population of 901. More than half of that increase occurred between 1910 and 1920 as African Americans began the Great Migration (1915–1940) from the South. Blacks were pushed from the South by racism, oppression, violence, and the boll weevil, which destroyed crops, and pulled to the North by promises of jobs, an end to discrimination, and more opportunities. Often, these promises did not materialize.

Dunbar's class was the last to graduate from Central High School. The school was torn down in 1893 and the Central District School was built. High school students began attending Steele at the southeast corner of Monument and Main Streets. The 1902 football team included George Wheeler. Courtesy of Wanda Sloan, goddaughter of George Wheeler.

Louise Troy, the daughter of Civil War veteran Samuel Troy and his wife, Mariah, taught in Dayton from 1878 until 1920. She began teaching in the old buildings on Ziegler and on Fifth at Baxter (Dunbar). She then moved to the the new Tenth District School on Fifth at Maple. After the schools were "integrated" in 1887 Louise Troy, the only African American teacher who was retained, taught at Garfield until 1920. Her pupils included Paul Laurence Dunbar, James Parsons, and William O. Stokes. Courtesy of Mrs. Viola Riffe Lloyd.

(Below) Garfield School at Fifth and Barnett was built in 1871. Though the frame building in which Louise Troy taught was removed in 1930, her influence remains, for she taught students to take their place as leaders in the community. She also taught future educators including Rosalie Dugger, Ella Lowry, Susan Shields, Ethel Stewart, Flossie Womack, and Nell Young. They served for many years in the Dayton Public Schools. Louise Troy Primary School at 1665 Richley Avenue, dedicated in 1959, honors this remarkable woman. Courtesy of the Dayton and Montgomery County Public Library.

(Left) Although he had graduated magna cum laude, *Paul Laurence Dunbar was refused a position on the local newspaper because he was black. He became an elevator operator, and continued writing. In 1892, using a loan from Dr. Henry Tobey, he published* Oak and Ivy. *In 1896, William Dean Howell's introduction to* Lyrics of a Lowly Life *helped make Dunbar a nationally known writer. Dunbar's success was bittersweet; he complained that publishers wanted only his dialect writings. Dunbar, a forerunner of the Harlem Renaissance, inspired Langston Hughes. Courtesy of the Dayton and Montgomery County Public Library.*

(Right) Dunbar, author of "A Toast to Dayton," is a vital part of Dayton's African American heritage. He wrote articles, musicals, novels, operettas, poems, and short stories. His talent made him and Dayton well-known. In 1897 he toured England as the guest of United States Ambassador John Hay. In 1899 he appeared in Boston with Dr. W. E. B. Du Bois and Booker T. Washington. Dunbar symbolizes the many African Americans who struggled, achieved, and contributed to Dayton and to the nation. Courtesy of the Dayton and Montgomery County Public Library.

Dunbar met Frederick Douglass at the Chicago World's Fair in 1893. His admiration for Douglass, who died in 1895, was expressed in "Frederick Douglass" and in "Douglass." Dayton's admiration for Dunbar, who died in 1906, was expressed by Dr. William Scarborough, president of Wilberforce University. "This beautiful city, the Gem City of Ohio, is proud to honor its famous son who has helped to give it fame—to honor him because of his worth, his genius, his work." (Scarborough, Address) Courtesy of the Ohio Historical Society.

1907 - 1951

1907 - 1926
Rev. J.B. Anderson

In 1892 Allen A.M.E. Church on Fitch Street, St. Margaret's Episcopal Church at Mound and Norwood, and Bethel Baptist Church on Dunbar (Baxter) were organized. Other churches organized during the first two decades of the twentieth century include Corinthian Baptist, Mt. Olive Baptist, Mt. Pisgah Baptist, Phillips Temple C.M.E., St. Paul A.M.E. Zion, Salem Missionary, and Summit Christian. Photographs courtesy of Bethel Baptist, Greater Allen A.M.E., and St. Margaret's Episcopal Churches.

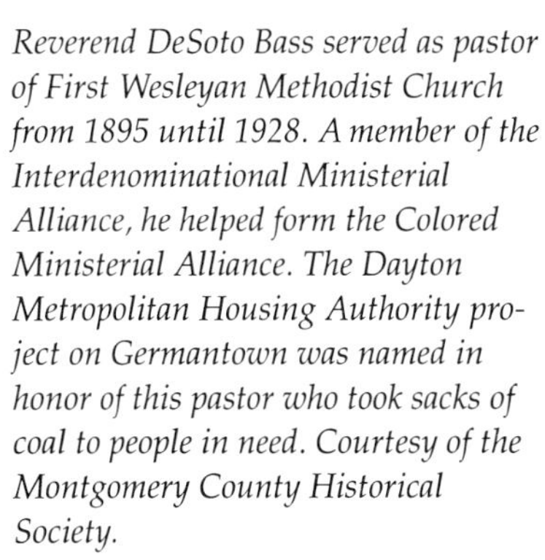

Reverend DeSoto Bass served as pastor of First Wesleyan Methodist Church from 1895 until 1928. A member of the Interdenominational Ministerial Alliance, he helped form the Colored Ministerial Alliance. The Dayton Metropolitan Housing Authority project on Germantown was named in honor of this pastor who took sacks of coal to people in need. Courtesy of the Montgomery County Historical Society.

YWCA work in the black community began about 1889. The program is the country's oldest continuously existing black YWCA. Louise Troy, Jessie Hathcock, and the other women who had organized the Women's Christian Association (WCA) No. 2 in the basement of the Eaker Street AME Church bought this house at Fifth and Horace in 1909. They later gave the West Side YWCA the use of the house. Courtesy of the Montgomery County Historical Society.

Jennie Cox, the wife of Dr. Lloyd Cox, also served as a leader in the West Area YWCA. Courtesy of the Dayton YWCA.

In 1914 Mary "Ma" Scott (1851–1919) determined to help aged black women. She called together a group of women and that November she opened her home as a shelter. The women went to the churches and from door to door seeking donations, which the community provided. In 1915 the Mary Scott Home opened in a rented dwelling on Dunbar Street. It later relocated to Germantown and Adelite, and then to Wolf Creek Pike. In 1928 the home was moved to 108 Garst Street. Drawing by Kenny Smith, courtesy of the Mary Scott Nursing Center, Inc.

Mary Shaw, another founder of WCA No. 2 and the YWCA, participated in the National Association of Colored Women's Convention at Wilberforce in 1914. When Mary died in 1929, Jessie Hathcock of WCA No. 2 and Lilla Rogers of the YWCA wrote a resolution praising her as one whose life was an inspiration. Courtesy of the Dayton YWCA. Courtesy of the Dayton YWCA.

(Below) Alberta Robinson and her family were living at Longworth and Mead when the flood began. As the water kept rising, Alberta, three siblings, a cousin, and Mrs. Robinson moved to the second floor. Mr. Robinson, unable to return home because of the high water, was standing on the trestle above Longworth. Two trains stopped on the trestle. He and the other men grabbed lumber that was floating by, made a raft, and used bellcords to guide the raft to the house. After the family crawled onto the raft, the men pulled it to the eastbound train, which moved on to Union Station. The family crawled onto the roof of the station and into the tower. Five-year-old Marjorie died from exposure. Courtesy of Alberta Robinson Sloan.

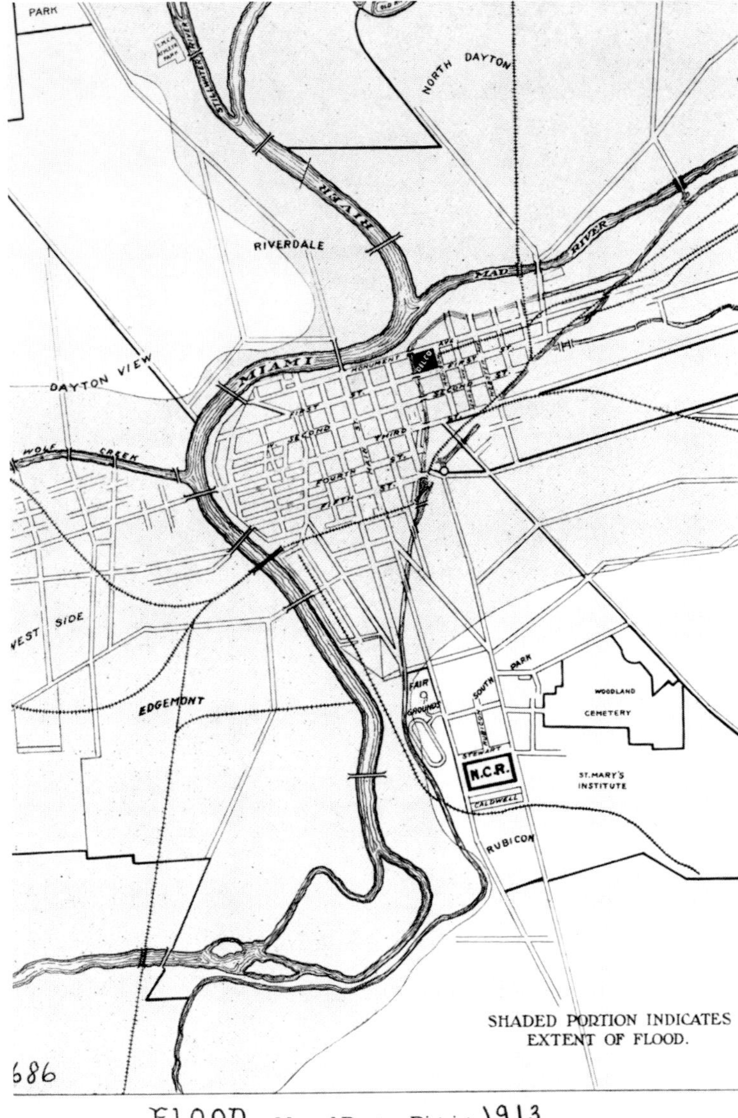

(Above) On March 25, 1913, the rain began. In three days, about 9,000 billion gallons of water fell on already water-soaked ground. (Montgomery County Historical Society, Going to the Source*) The flood covered much of Dayton with water from twelve to twenty feet deep, and killed seventy-nine people. Frank Thoro, George Crandall, and Marcos baseball team member William Sloan rescued 317 people, including William Irvin and his parents. They used a boat taken at gunpoint from an owner who was not using it, but would not loan it to others. (Bernstein, "The Colored Ball Player") Courtesy of the Dayton and Montgomery County Public Library.*

1876 — 1920

In the 1870s, according to the U.S. Census, 730 "colored males" (men of "negro descent, Chinese, Japanese, and civilized Indians") were employed. Of these, 250 were laborers and 180 were servants. The 276 employed colored females included 172 servants, 64 laundresses, and 7 laborers.

Although new occupations such as molder had appeared, and there were four professors and teachers, most colored Daytonians were in labor/service occupations.

The 1920 Census reported that 1,481 of the 3,712 employed Negro males were laborers in such areas as steel rolling mills, automobile factories, and the building trades. There were 852 in domestic and personal service. Of the 1,491 employed Negro females, 1,295 were in domestic and personal service.

There were twenty-seven clergymen, thirteen teachers, and eleven physicians; however, like the Adkins, most of the 5,203 employed black Daytonians were in labor/service jobs.

The 420 West Fifth Street home/office of Dr. Lloyd Cox (seated) was severely damaged by the flood. His brother Leroy, Dayton's first licensed black pharmacist, had not yet opened his drugstore. However, Dr. A. L. Biggs had to swim out of the flood as he was still in his office at 814 West Fifth Street. He lost everything and had to start all over again. Marianna Harris recalls her father carrying her across the Fifth Street bridge just before it collapsed. Courtesy of Reba Cox Gaston.

After her husband's death, Mrs. Johnson (page 8) remarried. This photograph, taken in about 1918–1919, shows Mr. and Mrs. Adkins at their home at Fifth and Dunbar (Baxter). Mrs. Adkins continued working as a laundress, and Mr. Adkins worked as a janitor. Like other parents, they worked hard so their children could have more opportunity than they had enjoyed. Juanita became a nurse and Irene became a teacher. Courtesy of Juanita Johnson Senior.

In 1910 George Wheeler became Dayton's third black police officer. The first two were William Jenkins (1897) and Lucius J. Rice (1909). This photograph shows the lone black officer, second from right, in 1915. During Prohibition, Wheeler heard bottles clink as a man wearing a trenchcoat walked along West Fifth Street. Wheeler asked the man what he was doing. The man answered, "Oh, nothing." Wheeler took his nightstick, smashed the bottles in the hidden pockets, and walked away as the man stood, dripping alcohol. Courtesy of Josephine J. Wheeler.

In 1917 Dr. Lloyd Cox moved into this home at 1301 Superior. He had the work done by African Americans: architect M. A. Pollett, builder Oscar Evans, cement contractor Charles Price, and foreman Ed Jackson. Dr. Cox donated his services to the American Red Cross and Linden Recreation Center, worked in Alpha Phi Alpha Fraternity's "Go to High School—Go to College" campaign, helped establish Dunbar High School, and served the community as a physician for fifty-seven years. Courtesy of Reba Cox Gaston.

This photograph of Dr. Lloyd Cox at his 420 West Fifth Street home/office was taken about 1912. Doctors Adolphus Biggs, James Bush, Emmett Campbell, Elijah Clemens, Lloyd Hathcock, Thomas Robinson, Charles Rogers, and B. Andrew Rose also had offices on West Fifth Street. Dr. William Taylor was at 304 South Williams, and Dr. Isaiah Turner was at 1143 Germantown. Courtesy of Reba Cox Gaston.

Mr. and Mrs. John Rives began publishing the Dayton Forum *in 1913. As the paper began its twenty-ninth year in 1941, Rives' editorial noted that the Negro population had grown from 3,000 to 30,000, but that the thriving West Side was not controlled by Negroes. Rives—like later black newspaper editors Charles Francis, Joseph Saunders, Lawrence Nelson, Ernie Bickerstaff, Harvey Simmons, Murray West, Jack Harris, and Don Black—played vital roles as both a source of information to the black community and a voice speaking for that community. Photograph by Edward Taylor, courtesy of William S. Johnson Jr.*

In 1910, Joseph Walter Shaw and his wife, Lucille, who had come to Dayton from South Carolina, established their first cleaning plant in an old building at 620 West Fifth Street. Their son, Joseph Shaw Jr., worked with them. Courtesy of Joseph Shaw Jr.

In 1911 James Dunn became the first African American to graduate from the Ohio State University with a degree in architectural engineering. His wife, Lulu Mae, was the first African American woman to graduate from Antioch's College of Music in Yellow Springs. She became a music teacher. James, Montgomery County's first black deputy engineer, designed many of the county's roads and bridges. He also designed the Alpha Phi Alpha Fraternity Shield. In 1942 Dunn became president of the National Technical Association. Courtesy of Dorothy Dunn Whiteside.

Joseph Shaw Jr. has retired, but his son, Joseph Whitfield Shaw, is the owner-manager of this plant at 2241 Germantown and of their new (1994) plant in Randolph Township. His grandsons, Christopher and Joseph Whitfield Jr., the fourth generation of this family of entrepreneurs, are learning the business. Courtesy of Joseph Shaw Jr.

Mrs. N. A. Anderson, owner of The Home Store at 324 Sprague Street, is remembered as a good businesswoman. An ad in the June 13, 1919, Dayton Forum *shows that she also had the spirit that helped the black community thrive. Her ad offered "FREE FOOD in case of sickness or accident." She was also active in the YWCA. Courtesy of the Dayton YWCA.*

(Below) W. A. Bell owned the Bell Hotel (right) at 320 South Ludlow. It opened in 1904 and was in operation until 1932. Robert Mallory opened the Mallory Hotel at 314 South Ludlow and managed it until 1912. It was later called the Palace (under H. Gardner and Brownie McDowell) and the St. Regis (under H. E. Williams and Chet Turner). The building was razed in 1932. Courtesy of the Dayton and Montgomery County Public Library.

In 1917 Eliza Louise Macmillan (right) came to Dayton from Tennessee, where she had been a teacher. In Dayton she became a hairdresser. She also met and married Con Waters, who is seen standing in front of the barber shop and beauty shop they established at 224 Dunbar in the late 1930s. Mrs. Waters, an officer in the Amarantha Grand Chapter of the Order of Eastern Star and a member of Greater Allen A.M.E. Church, was also a noted speaker, writer, and entertainer. Courtesy of Helen McGrew Hill and family.

In 1906, after attending the Columbus, Ohio, School of Mortuary Science with the encouragement of his employer Frank Resinger, Hazey P. Loritts established Dayton's first black-owned funeral parlor at 636 West Fifth Street. Loritts was president of the Dayton NAACP, Seventh Ward Republican Committeeman, and an active member of Wayman Chapel A.M.E. Church, the Masons, and the Elks. In 1994, the Loritts Funeral Home at 3924 West Dr. Martin Luther King Jr. Way became the Loritts/Neilson Funeral Home. Courtesy of Viola Lloyd.

In June 1918, E. T. Banks reported to Harper's Ferry, West Virginia, for two weeks training before going to France as YMCA Secretary. Banks had already helped make the Fifth Street Y the oldest incorporated "colored" Y in the country; begun Linden Center; served on the committee that rewrote the city charter; made his collection of biological specimens available to children; and served the community in other ways. While overseas, he earned the title "Fighting Secretary." After the war Banks often gave speeches about his wartime experiences. Joe Shaw Jr. recalls hearing him tell how the Germans dropped their guns and ran when the black troops came over the hill. Photograph by Baker, courtesy of George Banks, grandson.

THE DAYTON FORUM

Vol 6 Number 16 DAYTON, OHIO, FRIDAY SEPT. 20, 1918 Price 5 Cents

SOME OF THE SPEAKERS FOR EMANCIPATION DAY

ATTY. NORRIS

REV. MEADE

C. W. PRICE

MOSES H JONES

REV. DAY

This September 21, 1918, Emancipation Day celebration began at 9:00 A.M. with a parade to the Montgomery County Fairgrounds by Civil War veterans, Sunday School classes, and others. The program included a women's horse race, prayer by Reverend Day, the reading of the Emancipation Proclamation by Maud Walker, and a barrel race. The day ended with moving pictures and a dance at Memorial Hall. Everyone was urged to participate in honor of the 311,803 colored soldiers in the army during World War I. (Dayton Forum, *"Emancipation Day Program")*

NEGRO ATTORNEY IS DEAD AFTER SHORT ILLNESS

There were four black lawyers in Dayton between 1876 and 1920: Wayde Buydden, 1204 United Brethren Building, Fourth and Main, northeast corner; Moses Jones, Davies Building, Fourth and Main, southeast corner; Thomas Norris, Rauh Building, Fourth and Jefferson, southwest corner; and William Stokes, 346 West Fifth. A memorial committee, chaired by Judge Oren Brown, called Jones "the best colored criminal lawyer in Ohio." Ella Lowry remembered Jones as dark, very handsome, and dignified. He made such as impact on student Aurelia Turner that she decided all of her children would get a college education. The seven Turner children fulfilled her dream. (Dayton Daily News, *"Negro Attorney")*

Black Daytonians waged war on two fronts. Nannie Keith demanded justice for the black man who was fighting overseas, but was barred from working beside white Americans, and for herself, barred from theaters showing films of the war in which her own brother was fighting. Reverend J. N. Samuels Belboder (first row, right end) pastor of St. Margaret's Episcopal Church and president of the Dayton NAACP, sent an open letter to President Woodrow Wilson, reminding him that Earth and Heaven were tired of nations uttering insincere words of truth and justice. Courtesy of Eleanor Ramey.

Serg. Garfield W. Jones

Wishing all of his Friends
A Merry Christmas and
hopes to see them soon

JONES BROS. Undertakers
438 W. Fifth St. Bell Main 4189

The November 22, 1918, Dayton Forum *headline was "DAYTON BOYS IN THE BATTLE OF ARGONNE." Captain Robert Mallory (above)Leads Old Co. C in Sanguine Struggle With the Huns." The article praised the colored soldiers who, under Mallory's leadership, so splendidly maintained their line. The men of Company C and other black soldiers served despite the racism shown by white officers addressing black soldiers as "coon"; by the retirement of Colonel Charles Young to avoid having him lead troops; and by an official order instructing the French military mission not to deal with black officers "on the same plane as with the white American officer," and to keep the French people from spoiling the Negroes. (Bennett,* Before the Mayflower*) Courtesy of the* Dayton Daily News.

(Left) Garfield Jones, wounded in the Argonne Forest battle, opened his funeral parlor at 438 West Fifth Street in 1909. He was a member of Ancient Square Lodge No. 40, Lee Carpenter Post No. 328 of the American Legion, and Zion Baptist Church. He was also chairman of Troop 30, Boy Scouts of America. Robert Mallory attributed much of his success to Garfield Jones. Dayton Forum.

Dr. Arnold Shaw, seen here with the 1912 Steele High School track team, also participated in the battle in the Argonne Forest. He later served the Dayton community as a podiatrist. Many Daytonians also remember Dr. Shaw as the director/producer of musicals and plays such as A Rajah's Romance, *and as the star of* Death Takes a Holiday, *and other plays. Courtesy of Rebecca Shaw.*

During World War I, Reverend Charles Higgins served as secretary under the War Work Council of the YMCA. Mrs. Higgins, the great-granddaughter of Charity Broady, served for some time with her husband. Reverend Higgins entered Bonebrake Seminary after educating their children, and graduated when he was sixty-three. In 1951 Mrs. Higgins was honored by the YMCA as one of fifteen Pioneer Mothers. Johnson, First Wesleyan.

(Above) In 1994, as the Gettysburg/Lakeview area was being destroyed to make way for I-35, it was hard to realize that Lakeside Park had been there from 1890 until 1967. The park was very popular, but black people were not allowed in the Dance Pavillion and could ride only certain horses on the carousel. E. T. Banks charged that these restrictions had laid the foundation for attacks against black people on July 20, 1919. He encouraged "race people" to go to Lakeside fearless, because "fear enslaves body and soul." ("The Trouble at Lakeside," Dayton Forum*) Courtesy of the Dayton and Montgomery County Public Library.*

One leisure-time activity was baseball. These are the Dayton Marcos, one of the eight teams in the Negro National League, formed in 1920. Before 1920, the Marcos, who began playing in the early 1900s, were the only black team in the Ohio-Indiana League. Bill Sloan, a hero during the 1913 flood, is the first person standing on the left in this photograph taken at Westwood Field. William Ellis recalls crowds of Marcos fans walking from McCall Street to Westwood Field, now the site of Metro Market on James H. McGee Boulevard. Courtesy of Alberta Robinson Sloan.

Religion continued to play a major role in the lives of black Daytonians. Here Reverend T. J. Smith baptizes members of Zion Baptist Church during the 1920s. Churches established between 1921 and 1940 included Ethan Temple (Seventh Day Adventist); Macedonia, Mt. Calvary, Mt. Enon, Pleasant Hill, Shiloh, Sunlight, Tabernacle, and Zion Hill (Baptist); and Greater St. John Missionary Baptist. St. John the Baptist Catholic Parish, established in 1893, had become St. John the Baptist (Colored) Parish by 1938. Courtesy of Juanita Johnson Senior.

CHAPTER THREE

1921 – 1940

As the Great Migration continued, Dayton's African American population more than doubled, increasing from 9,025 in 1920 to 20,273 in 1940.

Black Daytonians participated in activities at the YMCA, YWCA, and Linden Center; began attending Roosevelt and Dunbar High Schools; beamed with pride when Avery Watson from Steele won honorable mention in the 1940 American Youth Forum in which almost 500,000 students participated; and celebrated Joe Louis's victory over James Braddock with a parade along Fifth Street.

They fought against discrimination. They participated in activities at Marcus Garvey Hall at Germantown and Williams, worked with the Dayton chapter of the Universal Negro Improvement Association (U.N.I.A.), and listened to Dr. W. E. B. Du Bois speak on "Democracy and the Darker Races."

They also endured the Great Depression, which followed the stock market crash of October 29, 1929. John Bowman was among the many laid off during this period. He started a coal and ice business, and insisted that his children continue their education.

St. Paul A.M.E. Zion was established in 1913 at a member's home on Eaton Avenue (McCall). In 1923 the congregation moved to the building at 1117 Home Avenue. Today, the congregation worships at 4544–50 Laurel Avenue. Courtesy of St. Paul A.M.E. Zion Church.

Marianna Harris summarized the impact of the Great Depression on black Daytonians. "So many people lost their homes, but they kept going. We're strong."

Members of Corinthian Baptist Church enjoyed a picnic at Hills and Dales Park in 1922. Corinthian was founded in 1915, and the congregation worshiped in Hathcock's Grocery Store at the corner of Eaton (McCall) and Western (James H. McGee). Today, the congregation worships in the same area, at 700 South James H. McGee Boulevard. Courtesy of Corinthian Baptist Church.

(Above) In 1932, members of McKinley United Methodist Church posed for this Children's Day photograph. The church's history can be traced to 1887, when Reverend J. H. Payne reorganized a mission on Hawthorn Street into the Hawthorn Street Methodist Episcopal Church. The name was changed to McKinley in 1895 in honor of the president. The congregation still worships at 196 Hawthorn. Courtesy of McKinley United Methodist Church.

(Left) The Fifth Street YMCA, 907 West Fifth, was opened to the public on New Year's Day, 1928. The honored guests were former chairmen of the Committee of Management Dr. Lloyd Cox and Lucius Rice, and former secretaries Reverend Edward Terrell Banks and Reverend Charles Higgins. Courtesy of the Dayton YWCA.

Those identified in this photograph taken in front of the Fifth Street YMCA in the late 1930s include, first row from left: (1) Norman Morris, (3) Pierce Gross, (5) Bobby Lewis, (6) Henry Heflin, (7) Beotus Phillips, (15) Donald Caesar, (18) Buddie Branch, and Lloyd Lewis Jr. Second row: (3) Earl Turner. Third row: (4) Bobby Fields, (10) Physical Education Director Lloyd Lewis Sr., (11) YMCA Secretary John Green, (16) Lon Chaney. Fourth row: (3) Robert Lee, (16) Lawrence Bowman, (20) Charles Huff, and (22) William Tanner. Fifth row: (13) Tunney Fisher, (14) Scoutmaster A. W. Payne, and (17) Al Tucker. Courtesy of Lloyd Lewis Sr.

SPIRIT
MIND
BODY
THE YOUNG MEN'S CHRISTIAN ASSOCIATION
BOYS

The members of this Black History class at the West Side YWCA around 1924 are standing in back of the building. Those identified include, from left: (1) Lula Clay, (2) Cornelia Lacy, (3) Mabel Brady, (5) Emma T. Smith, (6) Helen Gilliam, (7) Alice Marten, (8) Lilla Rogers, (9) Susie Reeves, (10) Irene Rollins, (12) Nora Dunn, (15) Susie Burleigh, and (16) Leota Rust. Courtesy of Zion Baptist Church.

(Right) Those identified on the YMCA's 4–6 team included, front row from left: (1) Rembert Stokes, (2) John Parsons, (3) Robert Stokes, (4) Lee Bowman, (5) Russell Patterson, (6) J. Paul Prear, and (7) Johnny Arnold. Standing: (2) Bill Jackson, (3) Warren West, (4) Leroy Green, (5) Mac Ross, (6) Buddy Webb, (7) Colie Cannon, (8) Carter Clark, (9) Henry Parks, and (11) Lloyd Lewis Sr. Courtesy of Lloyd Lewis Sr.

George Vaughn began going to the Y every week in 1930. There he came under the positive influence of Lloyd Lewis Sr. After he became a private pilot in 1947, Vaughn sent this thank-you photograph to Mr. Lewis, who helped so many young men. Courtesy of George Vaughn, Sky King.

A. W. Payne (fifth from left, first row) began Boy Scout Troop 30 at the "colored" Y at Third and Charter in 1919. Others identified in this 1932 photograph include, front row from left: (1) Robert King, (6) C. J. McLin Jr., and (7) Henry Smith Jr. Back row: (4) William Revere, (6) Edgar Nickerson, and (10) Henry Parks. In 1950, Henry Parks, founder of the Parks Sausage Company in Baltimore, Maryland, sent a donation to George Wheeler at the Y, with a letter stating he'd never forget Troop 30, the Fifth Street Y, or Scoutmaster Payne. Courtesy of Estella Hand.

The Delphinium Garden Club was organized in 1931 by Estella Hand, Georgia Johnson, Hattie Manson, Beulah Phillips, and Adah Turner. Members in this 1940s photograph are, seated left to right: Cora Gardner, Willa Matson, Emma Jackson, Ophelia Sebree, Drusilla Bass, and Fannie Fugett. Standing: Lucille Miller, Evelyn Robinson, Estella Hand, Arhoda Miller, Grace Moxley, and Hattie Manson. Club members have carried out neighborhood beautification projects and given seeds to children so they could have their own gardens. Courtesy of Estella Hand.

Bertie (Mrs. George) Ellis, known as Mom Ellis to thousands of young people, served the YWCA for ten years as membership and employment secretary, and as acting executive director. She also worked on the bond issue that helped build Linden Center and was director of women's and girls' activities for eleven years. She was the first president of Dayton's League of Colored Women Voters, organized in 1921. Mrs. Ellis also served on the Dayton Urban League Board and with other community groups. Courtesy of the Montgomery County Historical Society.

(Above Right) Mabel (Mrs. George Evens) served as chairman of the Committee of Management of the West Side YWCA. In 1932 she became the first black woman to serve on the Dayton YWCA's Board of Directors. Courtesy of the Dayton YWCA.

Marguerite Jefferson Manning, a member of Alpha Tau, was one of the sorors present when Beta Eta Omega Chapter of Alpha Kappa Alpha Sorority was chartered in 1934. The charter members were Jessie Hathcock, Carrie Shaw, Lucie Taylor, Ruth Wright, and Roberta Yancy. The Irma A. Pitman Scholarship Fund, established in 1994 to honor an outstanding educator, is one of the projects sponsored by the sorority. Photograph by Varden, courtesy of the the Manning family.

As this period ended, the U. S. Census showed that for the 3,984 employed Negro males, the top five categories were 1,407 service workers, 984 laborers, 668 operatives, 394 craftsmen, and 140 clerical/sales workers. Sixth place was a tie, 128 each in domestic and professional and semiprofessional work.

Almost ninety percent of the 2,105 employed Negro females were in the first two categories: 1,481 domestic service workers and 398 service workers, except domestic and protective. The 77 professional and semiprofessional women were the third category.

Thus, the majority of the black workers, like William Camp, were still in labor/service jobs; however, the number in professional and semiprofessional work was increasing.

Joseph Peters worked as a coal miner to pay his way through West Virginia Collegiate Institute, where he was an honor student and captain of the football team. After serving in the army, he came to Dayton in 1922 and became an independent contractor after a promised job vanished when the employer discovered he was black. Peters designed and built many homes in Dayton, including those at 2048 and 2051 Lakeview, and 500 Eleanor. He was a member of the NAACP and a trustee and Sunday School teacher at Zion Baptist Church. Courtesy of the Peters family.

(Right) The Great Migration continued. William and Estellar Camp came to Dayton from Hoschton, Georgia, in 1922. Mr. Camp, a laborer, helped build Roosevelt High School. The family lived at 313 Western. Ruth, the daughter, recalls seeing Native Americans in beautiful headdresses walking down the street. The Native Americans, having been displaced by white settlers, were the first residents of the West Side. Courtesy of Mrs. Ruth Camp Harris.

Like others who had come to Dayton seeking work, Joseph Peters sent for his family. His parents and five sisters and brothers, including Guy (right), came to Dayton. Arthur (left) chose to stay in Charleston. Guy helped build the Classic Theatre and worked as an usher. He also drove for Jack Spicer's West Side Cab Company and worked with Joseph. Courtesy of Guy Peters.

Velma Blair Morton, seen here as a senior at Steele High School in 1927, was the first black nursing supervisor in the Visiting Nurses Association, for which she worked from 1942 until 1974. She is a past president of the Ohio Nurses Association. Courtesy of Velma Blair Morton.

Dr. James Gunn, 314 South Western, was one of the many black doctors practicing between 1921 and 1940. The fifteen with offices on Fifth Street were Doctors Adolphus Biggs, James Bush, Emmett Campbell, Sanders Coston, Lloyd Cox, Donald Gillim, Lloyd Hathcock, Charles Johnson, Owen McFall, Russell Penman, George Pugh, Thomas Robinson, Charles Rogers, B. Andrew Rose, Washington Rowan, and A. Lynn Taylor. Doctors Maceo Clarke and Richard Price were at 1307 Germantown and 476 South Broadway, respectively. Courtesy of the Gunn family.

Three of the six black lawyers practicing between 1921 and 1940 had their offices on West Fifth Street: Matthew Shields, pictured here, was located at 837 $^{1}/_{2}$; Theo C. Carter at 903; and William O. Stokes at 449. Wayde Buydden and J. Gilbert Waiters were at 38 East Fifth; Thomas Norris at Fourth and Jefferson; and Herbert Morton, the first black graduate from the University of Dayton, at 118 Horace. Courtesy of the Montgomery County Historical Society.

Exine Prear began her distinguished career as a nurse in the 1930s. She was one of the first African American nurses at the Veterans Administration in Dayton, where she worked the night shift in order to care for her children during the day. She also worked with the city Health Department, served as a volunteer for the Red Cross, and worked with Dr. Adolphus Biggs, the first black physician hired to examine athletes in the Dayton Public Schools. Courtesy of Jeanette Prear.

Sanger Williams came to Dayton around 1920. He later worked as a chauffeur for U. S. Attorney General and Supreme Court Justice Frank Murphy until Murphy died in 1949. While working for the Justice Department, Williams served as chauffeur and private bodyguard for President Franklin Roosevelt. Williams died in Dayton in 1974. Courtesy of Mabel Williams.

Prilly Wright Jr., who came to Dayton from Georgia in 1919, met and married Olivia Melson. The Wrights are shown with their daughters Helen, Iula, and Hazel in 1930. Wright, a 33rd Degree Mason and a member of the NAACP and of the First Baptist Church of Ridgewood Heights, was an electrical contractor. Courtesy of the Carter family.

Thomas Leigh unloaded trains in a coalyard and later worked for three foundries: the Dayton Malleable Iron Company, Duriron, and GH & R. Mrs. Leigh worked at King's Restaurant and did day work. Their daughter, Inez Leigh Lewis, a custodian at Meadowdale High School for seventeen years, recalls that their East Dayton home at 309 Springfield, like many other homes in Dayton, had no indoor plumbing. Courtesy of Walter and Inez Lewis.

The Duriron Company, a foundry still in operation in 1995 at 450 North Findlay, was a major employer during this era. These 1938 Garage and Transportation workers are Cottrell Stewart, Walter Lewis, Cornelius Bridges, Edward Wright, and Melvin Lewis (garage foreman). Walter retired in 1976 after working at Duriron for forty-three years, as he did not want to surpass his father, who worked there for forty-four years. From the 1938 Duriron News, *courtesy of Walter and Inez Lewis.*

After earning his engineering degree from Renssaeler Polytechnic Institute in Troy, New York, James Parsons became the Director of Duriron's Research Laboratory. He supervised what was reportedly the only all-black laboratory staff in the country. Parsons earned eight patents for developing processes which made stainless steel possible. Because of his achievements, in 1928 Parsons received the Harmon Medal from Orville Wright in the first public program at the Fifth Street Y. Charles Kettering delivered the address. Parsons later taught at Tennessee State University, the Ohio State University, and Garfield Skills Center. Courtesy of the National Afro-American Museum and Cultural Center.

Clarence Smith founded the Smith Funeral Home in 1939. The business is still in operation at 368 South Broadway. Rachel Smith-Blye, the first African American woman licensed as a funeral director in Dayton, was also Dayton's second African American policewoman. However, the title in which she takes the greatest pride is "daughter-in-law of Reverend T. J. Smith of Zion Baptist Church." Drawings by Bill Evans, courtesy of Rachel Smith-Blye.

Education remained a top priority in the African American community. Dr. Charles Johnson, Professor of Art at both Central State and Wilberforce Universities in Wilberforce, Ohio, taught at the Dayton Art Institute in the 1920s. He also helped many of his students, including Kenneth Tate and Martha Gunn, obtain positions. Standing with Dr. Johnson is his sister, Blanche McPherson, a member of the Unique Study Club. Courtesy of Theresa Edwards.

Lucius J. Rice joined Dayton's police force in 1909 and was promoted to sergeant in 1916. In 1939 he, George Wheeler, and Detectives Bill Benner and Fred Smith went to 515 College Street to arrest a murder suspect. In the shooting that followed, Rice was hit. His son, teacher/historian Robert Rice, drove him to St. Elizabeth Hospital. Four days later, Detective Rice died. Courtesy of the Dayton Police Department.

Vivian Ashe (second from the left, first row) was in the first grade at Longfellow when this photograph was taken in 1927. She recalls the class walking to Grace United Methodist Church for Bible lessons. Mrs. Ashe taught in the Dayton Public Schools from 1960 until 1984. Courtesy of Mrs. LaMar Ashe.

(Below) In 1938, these first grade students at Garfield posed with their teacher, Mrs. Viola Riffe Lloyd, who later became the first principal of Louise Troy Primary School. The students identified include, seventh from the left, first row: Donald Day. Second row: (3) Anita Davis, (5) Eunice Peoples, (8) Francis Williamson, and (11) Doris Banks. Third row: (5) Mary Boykins, and (8) Lois Turley. Fourth row: (2) Charles Brown, (7) Henry Gober, (8) Albert Spears, and (10) John Gross. Courtesy of Viola Riffe Lloyd.

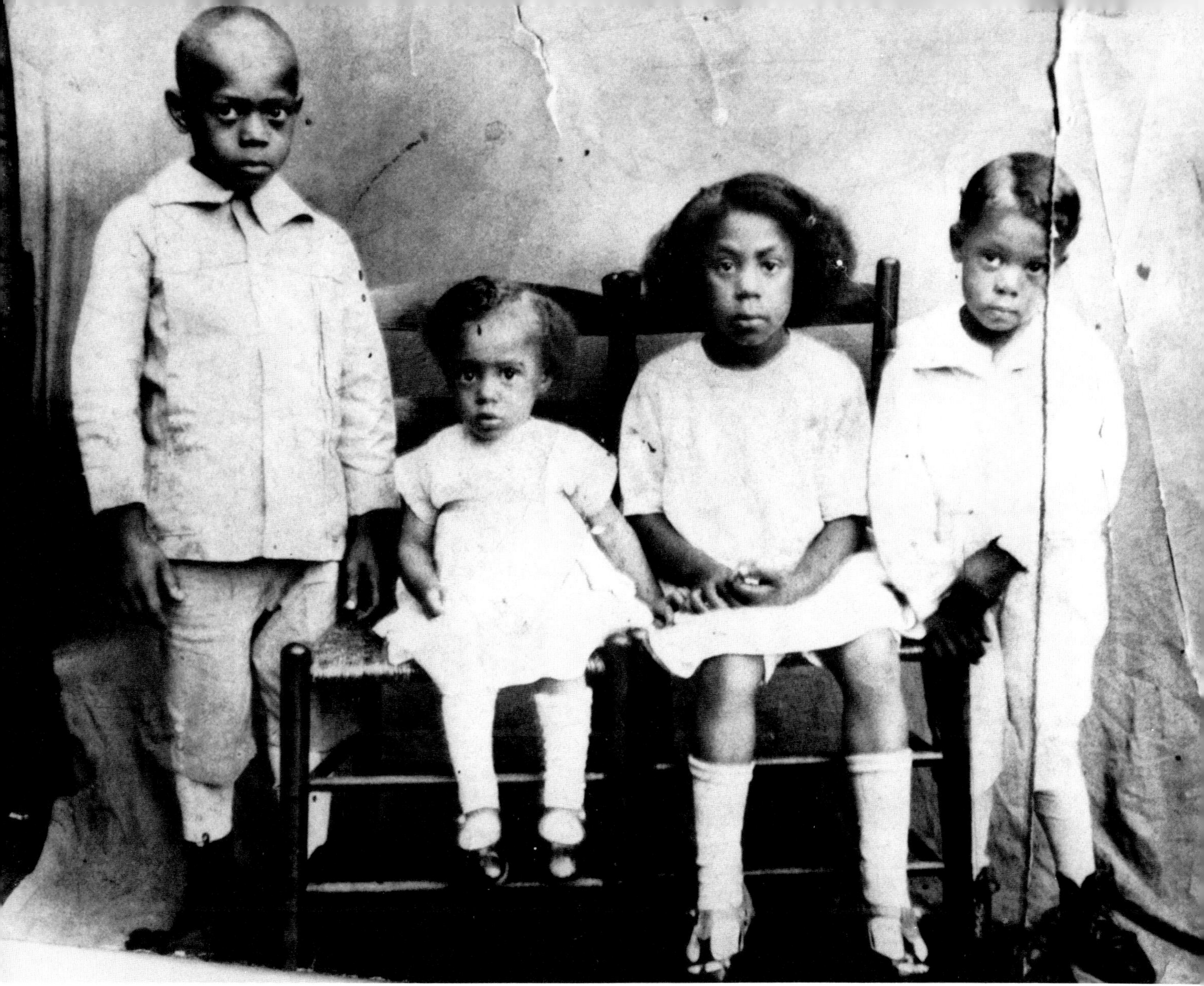

Rosalie Davis (third from the left), seen here with Major, Oziel, and Mitchell (Booty) Wood, attended Garfield. She remembers that in grades one through five, black students met in frame buildings and were taught by black teachers. In the sixth grade they went into the brick building with the white teachers and the white students. Courtesy of Rosalie Davis.

The Garfield staff in the 1940s included, front row: Maud Walker, Lillian Perry, Cora Robinson, Annabelle Carter, Ruth Mack, William Lansdown, Alexzina Gray, Virginia Early, Pearl Payne, Mildred Simmons, and Gladys Allen. Back row: Lawrence Jenkins, Ethel Garner, Herbert Pickens, Anne Samuels, Susan Shields, Viola Lloyd, William Quisenberry, Ella Lowry, and Joe Smith. Mrs. Lowry was born before the turn of the century. As a child she rode to Wilberforce in a horse-drawn carriage; as an adult, she went to Africa in a jet plane. Her contributions also spanned many years. She taught in the Dayton Public Schools from 1918 until 1965. At the age of 77, she began working with the Miami Valley Council on Aging. Courtesy of Mrs. Viola Riffe Lloyd.

In 1937 these fifth grade students at Willard, located at Summit and Germantown, posed with their teacher, Miss Gibson. The students identified include, front row from left: (2) Hortense Nelson, (4) Bessie Black, (5) Vivian Fletcher, and (8) Lonnie Wright. Second row: (2) Gerald Lovett, and (8) Donald Jackson. Third row: (4) Keria Gates. Fourth row: (1) Charles Revere. Fifth row: (1) Martha Irwin, and (2) Dorothy Favors. Courtesy of Ethel Gibson Wallace.

The Willard staff in 1937 included, front row, from left: (1) Almyra Oldwine, (2) Ethel Wallace, (3) Geraldyne Williams, (4) Charlotte Carroll, (7) Mildred Simmons, (8) Sirelda Sewell (also a WPA teacher), and (9) Margaret Irby. Second row: (1) George Tanner, (4) Marie Botts, (6) Nanette Shoecraft, (7) Wilma Sykes, (8) Maud Walker, and (9) Principal Mason. Third row: (1) Rosalie Dugger, (2) Edith Boston, (3) Florence Hall, and (4) Irene Jones, the baby in the Johnson family photograph in the preface. Courtesy of Ethel Gibson Wallace.

(Right) Ceola Brame of the Roosevelt Class of 1930, the national scholastic high jump champion, was the first black Daytonian to establish a national athletic record. Other local track stars include Amsden Oliver, who set a national record in the 220-yard high hurdles in 1931; David Albritton, silver medal winner in the 1936 Olympics; Lucinda Adams, gold medal winner in the 1960 Olympics; Craig Wallace, who broke Bob Hayes' 60-yard dash record in 1965; Edwin Moses, Olympic gold medal winner in 1976 and 1984; Chris Nelloms, winner of three gold medals in the World Junior Track and Field Championship meet in 1990; and Lavonna Martin, silver medal winner in the 1992 Olympics. Courtesy of Horace Brame.

(Below) The 1933–34 team was the first from Roosevelt to become state champions. Two African Americans, Charles Turley (left) and Al Tucker (right), were on the team. Courtesy of Al Tucker.

Roosevelt

1930

High School

(Above) The grouping of black students in this 1930 Roosevelt class picture is symbolic of the discrimination they encountered in a school whose principal, Mrs. Nettie Lee Roth, sent notes to Mrs. Clarence Bowman asking her to send her children to Dunbar. Separate swimming pools, separate dressing areas for athletes, and the denial of membership in the honor society led students such as Phyllis Blackburn (Greer) to transfer to Dunbar. Blonnie Jeter recalls more pleasant experiences, such as teachers staying after school to provide individual help. Courtesy of Robert Knoll Studio.

(Left) Mary Smith of the Roosevelt Class of 1930 had come to Dayton to attend school, as the all-black school she atttended in her native state of Virginia stopped in the seventh grade. She did day work and later worked at St. Elizabeth Hospital and in the county auditor's office. She loved to read and stressed education as a key to economic progress for black people. She was also an accomplished poet and speaker. In 1987 Dayton's Women for Racial and Economic Equality (WREE) honored her for her many contributions. In 1992 the Kwanzaa program at Roosevelt was dedicated to her memory. Courtesy of the Smith and Peters families.

(Right) Parental concern about Roosevelt being the only high school on the West Side and about the small number (less than one percent) of black teachers in the Dayton Public Schools led to the building of Paul Laurence Dunbar Junior High School. The school, located at 215 South Summit, opened in 1933 with an all-black staff and student body. Courtesy of the Dayton Daily News.

(Left) Ethel Stewart, Dayton's first black graduate librarian and the first black teacher elected to office in the Women's Educational Association, built Dunbar's library collection from 300 to 7,000 volumes. She was also chairman of the Y's Committee of Management. Courtesy of the Dayton YWCA.

(Above) Dr. John Harewood, second from the left in the first row, graduated from Wilberforce University magna cum laude *in 1932, but racial discrimination kept him from getting a job in the Dayton schools until 1938 at Dunbar. Dr. Harewood has served as a teacher, counselor, principal, and assistant superintendent. Also shown are other participants in the 1991 Martin Luther King Jr. School Awards Program. Front row: Reverend Jacque Franklin and State Representative Rhine McLin. Back row: Reverend Richard Duncan, Terra Ware, and Fred Bartenstein. Photograph courtesy of Newman Townsend Jr.*

(Far Right) Dr. F. C. McFarlane was Dunbar's first principal. Known for his belief in black people, he inspired those in his building and those he met in the community. When Dunbar opened in 1933, no funds had been provided for an athletic program; Chaminade Catholic High School of Dayton and Wilberforce University donated uniforms and other items. Because other Dayton Public School teams refused to play against them, the football and basketball teams had to travel out of the city to compete. Dr. McFarlane and David Albritton led the struggle against this racism. In 1950 Dunbar became a member of the Public School League. Courtesy of Robert Knoll Studio.

Dunbar High School 1936

(Above) Dunbar's first graduating class included future doctor Stanley Earley; educators Phyllis Blackburn, Virginia Buckner, and Lillian Revere; WAC Verniece Weir, and many others who would bring honor to their school and to their city. Courtesy of Robert Knoll Studios.

(Above) After he became successful as a writer, Paul Laurence Dunbar purchased this house at 219 North Summit. After Dunbar's death in 1906, his mother maintained the home as a shrine to her son. Volunteers such as Anne Givens, Ralph Jordan, Carrie Martin, and Eva Peterson devoted many hours to properly maintaining the home. Mother Dunbar died in 1934, and was buried next to her son at Woodland Cemetery. In 1938 the Dunbar home became a state memorial, with artifacts such as Dunbar's typewriter and the bicycle the Wright brothers gave him. The home is operated by the Ohio Historical Society, and tours are available. Courtesy of the Montgomery County Historical Society.

(Above) This photograph of the 1920–21 Marathons includes William Avery Jr., second from the left, front row. Back row: (1) Albert Jackson, (2) Theodore Thompson, (3) Dick Sloan, (4) Bill Sandridge, and (5) Wilcher Morton. The team of post-high school athletes began playing at Linden Center and was sponsored by the Supreme Liberty Life Insurance Company. Courtesy of Mrs. Lewis McGregor.

(Left) Sports continued to be very popular. Chester Blanchard, seen here in 1927, was shortstop for the Dayton Marcos from 1926 until 1930, when he retired as a player. Blanchard then worked as an umpire for about a year. Shortly after that, the Marcos disbanded. Blanchard worked for the Sunshine Biscuit Company from 1936 until 1969. Courtesy of Chester Blanchard.

(Right) Former Marathon members include, front row, from left: (1) Jimmy Jones Jr., (3) Clarence Lewis, (4) Bob McClellan, (6) Lewis McGregor, and (7) E. Frank James. Back row: (2) Harris Parrish, (3) Elijah Kilborn, and (6) Al Smith. Courtesy of Mrs. Lewis McGregor.

Members of Factory Service Team in Major Softball League

(Above) *Like many other Dayton factories, Frigidaire had a softball team in the Industrial League. In 1936, this Frigidaire team won the league championship. The players were, front row: Benny Franklin, Charles Stokes, Myron Glover, Johnny White, Jackie Fields, "Rock" Ferguson, "Bus" Fields, and manager "Weepy" Williams. Back row: "Ace" McKinney, Albert "Applejack" Drake, Ray Rollins, Johnny Arnold, Jack Jackson, Eugene "Dippy" Reid, Theodore "Razor" Christian, and Benny Pate. Courtesy of Charles Stokes.*

(Above) In 1940 Al Tucker began playing for the Harlem Globetrotters. The team members were Roosevelt Hudson, Tony Payton, C. Ford, Duke Cumberland, Al Tucker, and Charles Young. Tucker was also a member of the Jones Brothers Morticians Midwest League Basketball team, which included A. J. Drake, Tunney Fisher, William Jones, "Ace" McKinney, Red Prear, and Charles Turley. Jones Brothers teams won the city championship in 1947, 1949, and 1952. Hutchison Photo Service, courtesy of Al Tucker.

(Above) Duriron also had a basketball team in the Industrial League. The members of the 1938 team were, front row: Edgar Moore and Johnny Carpenter. Middle row: Aurelius Harbert (foreman, Induction Iron Melting Department), Melvin Evans, Walter Lewis, and John Slaughter. Back row: Rob Jackson and Alexander Crawford. Courtesy of Walter and and Inez Lewis.

Hartfield's

Anderson E. Mumford was among the black Daytonians who endured the Great Depression. Mumford's Dry Cleaners at 836 West Fifth Street was also the Mumford family's home. The business failed during the Depression, and the family had to move to Pease Street. Mumford became a watchman at the Dunbar Street railroad crossing in order to support his family. Courtesy of Jennie Mumford Swann.

Preceding Page:
(Top Left) Clarence Josef McLin Sr. (front, at the funeral of Reverend H. Laurence McNeil at Zion Baptist Church) was a leader in the business community with his funeral home at Germantown and Krug. McLin was also prominent in the political arena with his leadership in the Democratic Party. People he helped learn to register and vote formed the cadre of the Democratic Voters League. In 1938 McLin supported the Dayton Youth Movement in its demonstrations aimed at forcing West Side merchants to hire black people. McLin continued his work despite the bombing of his home. C. J. McLin Jr., in the center of the last row, worked closely with his father. Courtesy of State Senator Rhine McLin and family.

(Far Left) Ethel Prear was a dominant figure in the area of politics and human rights. She came to Dayton from Tennessee in 1923 and began to work in the NAACP, the Elks, the Republican Party, Greater Allen A.M.E. Church, and other organizations. She was the first black woman in Dayton to run for public office (the Dayton Board of Education) and the first to attend a Republican National Convention. Courtesy of Jeanette Prear.

(Left) The Reverend H. Laurence McNeil was also involved in the human rights struggle. He worked with the Dayton Youth Movement and was praised for a speech he gave rebuking "spineless leaders" who were afraid to stand up and defend black people. In 1947 Reverend McNeil became one of the first directors of the newly organized Dayton Urban League. Photo by Hartfield, courtesy of Zion Baptist Church.

(Above) Reverend E. T. Banks, his wife, Mary, and Dave West (right end) stand in front of the Banks' Upshaw Mission at McCabe and Blanche with residents of "Tintown." The name referred to the tin homes in which many of the 800 residents of this area lived. The mission led in planting vegetable gardens and canning food. In 1933 Banks represented Dayton's Home View Unit at a meeting in Washington, D.C. His practical suggestions of ways to deal with economic problems, and his address at the Workers and Farmers Convention in Columbus led to his election to the state executive committee of Workers and Farmers. Courtesy of George Banks, grandson.

(Right) Paul Harris Jr. remembers his father, pictured here, driving him and his mother to different banks, repeating, "That's closed." His father lost money in several banks. Despite his losses, Paul Sr. helped others by using his cocktail bar/restaurant at 1012–1014 West Fifth Street as a soup kitchen. Mrs. Marianna Harris's brothers, Hubert and Howell Elliott, lost their jobs as pages at the courthouse and became Works Progress Administration (WPA) workers. Hubert continued his education and became a teacher at Dunbar. Courtesy of the Harris and Parsons families.

Millwright Murray Hand, seen here with his wife, Estella, was among the many whose jobs were far from their homes. He rode a bicycle from his home on Pontiac in Edgemont to his job at the Advanced Foundry (now the WCC Foundry) at 107 Seminary, off the 1200 block of Huffman in East Dayton. During the Depression, he hunted and fished. The family had a garden and raised chickens, so they ate well. Courtesy of Mrs. Estella Hand.

Shown in photograph, FIRST ROW: John Howard, Vernon Daniels, Robert Kimble, Leroy Woods, Ralph Warner, George Vaughn, SECOND ROW: Charles Edwards, Richmond Jackson, Eugene Crockett, Robert Strickland, Curtis Bell, Lester Jones, William May, Samuel Largent, Leo Burgin, Raymond Kelly. THIRD ROW: Robert Wilson, Raymond Hines, Fred Tuggle, Clyde Hough, Beverly Allen, Fredrick Jackson, Joe Sanders, Henry Bailum. FOURTH ROW: John Day, Curtis Walker, Merrill Nared, Ernest Williams; Joe Gadson, Edward Fuller, John Mitchell, Fred Bullock, John Bedell.

George Vaughn (first row, right end) was among the Daytonians who found work in the Civilian Conservation Corps (CCC). The all-black Company 588 worked on park projects at Carillon Park and at the Englewood, Huffman, and Taylorsville Reservations. They built bridges, shelter houses, park roads, and drinking fountains, and did other useful work. George's father was among the WPA workers who helped repair the Washington Street bridge. Both the CCC and the WPA were New Deal programs designed to help ease unemployment during the Depression. Courtesy of George Vaughn.

During World War II, the three adult sons of Otto and Ethel Blackburn were in the Army. In the front row are Amelia and Dan. Middle: Betty, Otto, Ethel, and Otto Jr. Back: Phyllis, Randolph, Kenneth, Robert, and Imo. In 1965 Robert became a state senator (Democrat), representing the Third District. His death that year in an automobile accident ended a career that began with service as a member of St. Margaret's Episcopal Church and Alpha Phi Alpha Fraternity. Phyllis became a teacher, a principal, and the first African American woman employed as a director by the Dayton Public Schools. Courtesy of Phyllis Blackburn Greer.

CHAPTER FOUR

1941 – 1960

From 1941 to 1960, Dayton's total population increased from 210,718 to 262,332; the African American population increased from 20,273 to 57,288. As the first year of this period drew to a close, American involvement in World War II led to black Americans fighting the enemy and segregation both overseas and at home, just as they had done in every previous war. Rationing, Victory Gardens, War Bonds, and women working as machinists were part of the homefront scene.

During this period, black Daytonians attended the new Regal Theater, 1314 Germantown, with "all colored employees"; went to Cincinnati to see Jackie Robinson and the Dodgers; saw the emergence of new local human rights leaders including Reverend Cody Bush, W. S. McIntosh, Reverend David Gilbert, and the Southern Christian Leadership Conference (SCLC); witnessed the National Cash Register (NCR) opening its apprenticeship program to black people in 1958; and were reminded of the extent of discrimination in housing when the *West Dayton Profile* reported that ninety-five percent of Dayton's black population lived in West Dayton in 1960. West Dayton extended from the Miami River (the Third Street bridge) west and south to the city corporation line, and north to that line and Wolf Creek.

Corporal Buddie Branch was a member of the 761st Tank Battalion, the first black tank battalion to see action in World War II. Branch was decorated for bravery in France. Branch established covering fire for seventeen walking wounded and then dismounted from his tank. Despite heavy enemy fire, he inspected six disabled tanks and helped remove and evacuate seven litter cases. He carried each one approximately three hundred yards to shelter. The feat took four and a half hours, during which time the tank column was under intense fire from 88mm guns, machine guns, mortars, and snipers. Courtesy of Buddie Branch.

Charity Adams Earley was the first black woman to be commissioned as an officer in the Women's Army Auxiliary Corps (WACs). One Woman's Army *tells of her struggle against the racism and the sexism she and the women in her battalion encountered. In 1991 Charity was honored as Montgomery County's Citizen of the Year for her volunteer work, which included serving as a member of the Sinclair Community College Board of Trustees, and chairing the Parity 2000 Committee. In 1993 she was inducted into the Ohio Veterans Hall of Fame. Courtesy of Charity Adams Earley.*

Walter Lewis received his airplane mechanics training in Lincoln, Nebraska, and his training to serve overseas in South Carolina. He was with the 553rd Fighter Training Group, which was attached to the 332nd Fighter Group, under the leadership of Lieutenant Colonel Benjamin O. Davis Jr. Courtesy of Walter and Inez Lewis.

When Arthur Fisher joined the Army Air Corps, he served with black lawyers and others who encouraged him to further his education. Fisher was a second lieutenant in the 477th Bombadier Squadron. His protests against discrimination in the military led to his arrest, which increased his determination to be treated fairly. After the war, Fisher became the first black judge in the Montgomery County Court of Common Pleas. Arthur O. Fisher Park commemorates his many contributions to the Dayton community. Courtesy of Arthur O. Fisher.

All five Bowman brothers served in the armed forces during World War II. Shown with their mother are Lawrence, J. C., Ernest (seated on the floor), Lee, and Clarence. When Lawrence and another black Marine recruit left for camp, they had to travel on a bus by themselves, not with the other recruits. Lawrence fought at Iwo Jima and was awarded the Purple Heart. Courtesy of the Bowman and Martin families.

(Right) George Cooper, in the middle of the second row, was one of the Golden Thirteen, the first African American men commissioned as ensigns in the U. S. Navy in 1944. After the war, Cooper served as Housing Inspector and as Senior Planner and Expediter in the Dayton Department of Planning. He is most proud of having founded the Dayton Fund for Human Rehabilitation. Courtesy of George Cooper.

(Left) Gertrude Ivory-Bertram was with the first group of black professional nurses who served overseas. In 1943 and 1944 she served in Monrovia, Liberia. Nurse, the Story of One Woman's Effort to Succeed, *tells how her family's support and her faith in God helped her overcome many hardships. Courtesy of Mrs. Gertrude Ivory-Bertram.*

(Left) Pfc. Leroy Stokes, a former member of Dunbar High School's basketball team, joined the service in October 1942. He was killed in action in February 1944, having served overseas since December 1943. Dunbar students planted a tree at the school in his honor. Courtesy of Charles Stokes.

(Below) Lloyd Hathcock, at the U. S. Air Force Museum at Wright-Patterson Air Force Base, is standing in front of a P-47, the type of plane he flew as one of the Tuskegee Airmen. In May 1944, his plane was forced down and he spent eleven months in a Nazi prisoner of war camp. After the war, Hathcock worked with the 4950th Test Wing Wright-Patterson Air Force Base. Courtesy of the Dayton Daily News.

George Weaver, seen here with Labor Secretary Arthur Goldberg, President John F. Kennedy, and an unidentified man, was a member of the War Relief Commission of the Congress of Industrial Organizations (CIO). Weaver, who had attended Roosevelt High School and Howard University, served as Assistant Secretary of Labor for International Affairs from 1961 until 1969. Courtesy of Mrs. Dorothy Weaver.

(Above) Housing was a critical issue during the World War II era. The DeSoto Bass Courts on Germantown Street, built by the Dayton Metropolitan Housing Authority, were one response to the need for housing. This photograph shows Bruce Bolden at the segregated apartment complex in the 1940s. Former residents of DeSoto Bass include Dayton Contemporary Dance Company founder Jeraldyne Kilborn Blunden and Major General Frederick Leigh. Photograph by Norman Stroud.

(Above) Five years after World War II ended, the United States became involved in the Korean War. John Mitchell (right), seen with Charles Davis, served in Korea in 1951–52 as a member of the 452nd Bomber Group. Of the 450,000 Americans who served in the war, 54,246 were killed, 103,284 were wounded, 8,182 were missing in action, and 7,000 were prisoners of war. Local figures are not yet available, but James Snyder, president of the Korean War Veterans Memorial Support Group, is working to identify Daytonians who served so that they can receive the honor they deserve. Courtesy of John Mitchell.

The officers of the South Side Civic Association (SSCA) were (seated) Ethel Cain, Laura Bailey, and Gussie Bradley. Standing: Reverend Ollie Mapp, Jessie Perry, Fred Bowers, and Archie Johnson. In 1942 they and other residents of Benn's Platt, a half-square mile site now occupied by Welcome Stadium, lacked many basic services. By 1944, after organizing and going to the City Commission twenty-seven times, they had mail delivery, telephones, and hard-surfaced streets. When the land was condemned because the Miami Conservancy District planned to use it, the residents went to court and got a fair price for their homes. Many bought homes and farms in Dayton. Courtesy of the Honorable Fred Bowers and Mrs. Marguerite Bowers.

In 1940 and 1941, ads for homesites on "the most beautiful hill in Dayton" appeared in the Dayton Forum. *Homes began to be built in Clifton Heights, the area west of Clifton Drive betwen McCall and Lakeview. As the black population continued to move west, more homes were built. One was the Harold Mitchell home at 5 Kimberly Circle , built by J. A. Peters. In 1994, Mitchell, who still lives in the home, praised Peters' ingenuity and precision. He declared, "If you wanted to learn, he was the one to teach you the right way." Courtesy of the Peters family.*

In 1950 Republican Fred Bowers (right) became the first black person in Montgomery County elected to the state legislature. Democrat C. J. McLin Jr. (left) was elected to the Ohio House of Representatives in 1966. Bowers was on the committee that initiated the Fair Employment Practices Commission. McLin founded the Black Elected Democrats of Ohio. Both men were entrepreneurs. The Bowers Real Estate Company at 1712 West Dr. Martin King Jr. Way, and the McLin Funeral Homes at 1108 Germantown and 2108 North Gettysburg are still operating today. Courtesy of the Honorable Fred Bowers and Mrs. Marguerite Bowers.

(Far Right) The West Dayton Area Council (WDAC) was organized in 1954 under the leadership of long-time human rights activists Roselle and Donald Ellis. The WDAC's goal was to represent West Dayton neighborhoods and promote physical and social improvements. Its activities included improvement of municipal services such as code enforcement and voter registration drives. By 1967 the council included over 150 block and civic clubs and fifteen neighborhod associations. The council's activities became a part of the Model Cities Program. Courtesy of Roselle Ellis.

(Above) The Dayton NAACP continued the struggle for human rights. The organization helped secure the admittance of Negro maternity cases to St. Elizabeth Hospital and end discrimination in downtown theaters. Elizabeth Holloway had been arrested in 1939 when she tried to buy a ticket at Loews. In 1945, the staff of the civil rights organization included, front row: W. G. Sherard, president; Miley O. Williamson, executive secretary; Dr. Maceo Clarke, membership chairman; and Fred Bowers, vice president; Back row: Walter Floyd, C. J. Francis (labor and industry chairman, who also used his newspaper, the Dayton Citizen, *to advance the struggle), T. P. Turner, and Lavern Wilson. Courtesy of the Honorable Fred Bowers and Mrs. Marguerite Bowers.*

In 1954, W. S. McIntosh, the first marcher, began leading demonstrations against the city of Dayton, banks, and stores, demanding fair treatment and equal employment opportunities for black Daytonians. The second marcher is Reverend Walter Dunson, who began working with McIntosh as a teenager. McIntosh's efforts secured jobs and loans, but they also led to the loss of his dry cleaning business when suppliers refused to sell to him. He continued the struggle, opening his House of Knowledge bookstore in Westown. McIntosh was killed in 1974, while trying to stop a robbery in downtown Dayton. Courtesy of Reverend Walter Dunson.

The Board of Directors of the Dayton Urban League, organized in 1947, included C. J. McLin Sr., Lloyd Lewis Sr. A. B. Sacks, Anthony Haswell, and Mrs. James Parsons. One goal was ending discrimination in employment in Dayton. Through the league's efforts, Syble Hurt Anderson became the first black nurse in training at Miami Valley Hospital; Nellie Peniston the first black Ohio Bell service representative; Raymond Shackleford the first black apprentice electrician at General Motors' Moraine Products Division; and Don Ellis the first black fireman in the Dayton Fire Department. They paved the way for others; by 1951 there were six black firemen in Dayton. (Dayton Urban League, "Pioneers") Courtesy of the Dayton Daily News.

Religion continued to be an important part of African American life. Macedonia Baptist Church was founded in 1947. Reverend Marcus Clark, pastor from 1950 until 1993, is seen in 1958 at the 262 Hanover location. The members now worship at 27 North Gettysburg. Other churches founded between 1941 and 1960 include Dixon United Methodist (UM), Friendship Baptist, Greater Mount (Mt.) Nebo Missionary Baptist (MB), Harris Memorial Christian Methodist Episcopal (CME), New Zion Baptist, Philippi MB, St. Peters MB, Trinity United Presbyterian, and Westwood First Reformed African Methodist Episcopal (AME). In addition, Elijah Muhammad established a mosque at Germantown and Williams. Courtesy of Johnnie Mae Miller.

In 1950 Reverend E. R. Meriwether (center) became the pastor of the thirty-five-year-old First Baptist Church in West Carrollton, Ohio. He saw the need to relocate the church. In 1964 the congregation bought the building at 30 South Oberlin, and the church was renamed First Thessalonians Missionary Baptist Church. The pastor's family, in the front row, included (1) John Jr., (2) Gregory, (3) Valerie, (4) Vickie, and (5) Denise. Second row: (2) Norma and (5) Mrs. Meriwether. Third row: (3) Kate and (4) Roy. Fourth row: (4) Bernice, (5) Betty, and (6) Wilma. Last row: (1) Manuel and (4) Eugene. Courtesy of Kate Meriwether West.

The Vacation Bible School staff at Summit Christian Church on Norwood and Sprague included, front row: Mrs. Moore from Mt. Pisgah, Annie Laurie Harris, Sarah Butler, and Christina Johnson. Back row: Ethel Wallace, Lula Butler, Anne Owens, Reverend Eli W. Wilbert, Viola Riffe Lloyd, Betty Dugger-Ferguson, and Mrs. Wilbert. Courtesy of Ethel Wallace.

(Above) In 1952 Reverend J. Welby Broaddus became the first African American elected to the Dayton Board of Education. Dr. Broaddus, pastor of Tabernacle Baptist Church, is shown holding the shovel at the groundbreaking ceremony for the new building. Others in the photo include, front row: (2) Martha Sewell, (3) Reverend Gentry Worth, and (4) Reverend W. M. Carter. Photograph by Charles Underwood, courtesy of State Senator Rhine McLin and family.

(Right) The fire at St. Margaret's Episcopal Church on Norwood and Sprague in 1952 destroyed the building, but not the Chalices, the Reserved Sacrament, or the faith of the members. By 1961, Earl Rollins, Mrs. Mary Robinson, and Dr. Joseph Hickerson were able to burn the mortgage on their new building at 3010 McCall Street. Courtesy of Eleanor Ramey.

Shown in this photograph are participants in the 1950 Men's Day Celebration at First Wesleyan Methodist Church. Those identified include, front row: (1) Ed Harris, (2) Albert Miller, (3) Leroy Logan, (6) Robert Oldham, (7) William Johnson Sr., (8) William Shoecraft, and (9) Robert Johnson. Middle row: (1) Herbert Gates Sr., (2) Herbert Gates Jr., (3) Sam Coatney, (4) Paul Smith, (5) Dale Wright, (7) Jewell Wilson, and (8) Mose Chambers. Back row: (1) James Wilson, (3) Reverend Clarence Pauley, (4) Elder Rita Lee, (5) Reverend James Wilson, (6) Reverend William Dugger, (7) Robert Clark, and (8) Harold Wright. Photograph by Edward Taylor, courtesy of William Johnson Jr.

Shiloh Baptist Church traces its origin to a prayer band which first met at 370 Springfield Street in the home of Deacon and Sister Hansbro. The church was chartered in 1927, and the first church building was at Finley and Pruden. In 1941 the congregation moved to 137 Sprague. The choir in this photo is in that building. Since 1961, the congregation has worshiped at 3801 Fairbanks. Courtesy of Mrs. Harvie Brame.

Mt. Calvary Baptist Church was founded in 1934. The congregation is seen here in the 1940s, in front of the church at Groveland and McCabe. Reverend David Mundy is standing next to the sign. The congregation now worships at 3300 West Dr. Martin Luther King Jr. Way. Courtesy of Mt. Calvary Baptist Church.

Mt. Olive Baptist Church began in 1903 when members of a mission from Zion Baptist Church met at 918 Germantown. In 1913, they purchased a lot at 502 Pontiac. While the church was being built, the congregation met in a house on Homestead Avenue. In 1944 Reverend David McFarland (center), shown with the Baptist Young People's Union (BYPU) in the 1950s, became the pastor. Photograph by Jimmy Terry, courtesy of Mt. Olive Baptist Church, Reverend T. H. McFarland Jr., Pastor, and Reverend David McFarland, Pastor Emeritus.

PROGRESSIVE CLUB

Deacon Zack Mundy, President

Mrs. Nina Jones, Secret:

(Above) These are the members of Mt. Enon Baptist Church's Progressive Club in 1953. Mt. Enon began as a mission at Home Avenue and Hawthorn Street in 1925. That same year the members moved to South Summit. After worshiping in a small building at Germantown and Bank, and in a larger edifice at College and Mercer, the congregation now worships at 1501 West Dr. Martin Luther King Jr. Way. Courtesy of Gladys Poole, Mt. Enon Baptist Church.

(Left) St. John the Baptist Catholic Parish was established in 1893 by German families, who built this church at Hartford and Williams. After the 1913 flood, many families moved out and African Americans moved in. Black children attended the school, which was next to the church. The children in this 1950s photograph are taking part in a school mass. In 1963 the church and the school were razed to make way for Route 35. The parishioners now worship at St. Agnes, Resurrection, and St. James. The organ in the photograph is now at St. James. Courtesy of the Archdiocese of Cincinnati and St. James Catholic Church.

In 1957 Reverend Walter Dunson (second from the left in the first row) established Greater Mt. Nebo Missionary Baptist Church in a one-room building at 641 Birwood Avenue. A year later, the building was condemned, so he rented a building at 164 Colgate. The congregation built their new church at 172 Colgate without taking out a bank loan. Photograph by Charles Underwood, courtesy of Reverend Walter Dunson.

In May 1931, a mission was established by a group of black Daytonians who gathered with the intention of becoming a Baptist church. After completing the required probation period, the mission adopted the name St. Luke Baptist Church, and called Reverend David Revere as the first pastor. The storefront at Hawthorn and Gale in which the congregation worshiped was destroyed by a tornado. After worshiping at a building on Sprague Street and two other locations, in 1947 the congregation purchased land at Clifton and Lakeview, the site of the present church. The choir shown is at the Sprague Street church. Courtesy of St. Luke Baptist Church.

In 1945, the members of Wayman Chapel A.M.E. Church, located at Fifth and Bank Streets, dedicated their new organ. Seated on the right end is the Right Reverend Reverdy C. Ransom, D.D., Bishop of the Third Episcopal District. Next to him is Reverend Granville Reed. Photograph courtesy of Madalene Norris.

(Far Left) New Zion Baptist Church was founded in 1948 by Reverend William Howard French, who is shown with his wife, Mary Louise. The congregation first worshiped at 2637 Middle Avenue. It now worships at 141 North Upland. Courtesy of Reverend William Wilson.

(Above)Dixon United Methodist Church was organized in 1950. In 1951, the congregation posed for this photograph, taken at their church on McArthur between Germantown Street and Nicholas Road. The congregation now worships at 1691 Infirmary Road. Courtesy of Dixon United Methodist Church.

(Right) In 1923, the Second Seventh-day Adventist Church was organized by sixteen charter members. After meeting in a small building at Home and Western Avenues, the congregation purchased a church on South Williams in 1926. The members in this 1944 photograph are at that building. In the 1940s, the name of the church was changed to the Ethan Temple Seventh-day Adventist Church. Since 1963, the congregation has worshiped at 4519 Oakridge. Courtesy of the Ethan Temple Seventh-day Adventist Church.

FIRST OFFICERS OF TRINITY U.P. CHURCH

In November 1948, Trinity United Presbyterian Church was organized by its first pastor, Reverend James I. Davis, who served the church until his retirement in 1993. The first services were held in the DeSoto Bass auditorium. In 1952 the congregation purchased land at Fleetfoot and Lakeview; the cornerstone for the new church was laid in April 1953. Courtesy of Trinity United Presbyterian Church.

(Far Left) Harris Memorial C.M.E. Church was organized on January 26, 1947, by Reverend Harry Phillips Porter, D.D., Presiding Bishop of the Second Episcopal District of the Ohio Annual Conference, as a memorial to Reverend H. E. Harris. The first services were held in Smith's Memorial Chapel at 368 South Broadway. In November 1947, the congregation moved to its new home at 601 Germantown. It remained there until the construction of Interstate 75 forced it to relocate in 1962. Since that date, the congregation has worshiped at 1100 Kammer. Courtesy of Eloise Waites.

1941 — 1960

According to the 1960 census, as the period from 1941to 1960 ended, the top five categories for the 14,271 employed "non-white" males were 3,578 operatives (skilled laborers, as in a factory), 2,452 laborers, 2,442 service workers (except domestics), 1,935 craftsmen and foremen, and 1,135 clerical workers. The top five categories for the 9,724 females were 2,660 service workers, 2,502 private household workers, 1,879 clerical workers, 769 operatives, and 624 professional and technical workers.

For the first time, less than half of the black workers were in labor/service jobs. The rapidly changing job-market called for skilled workers.

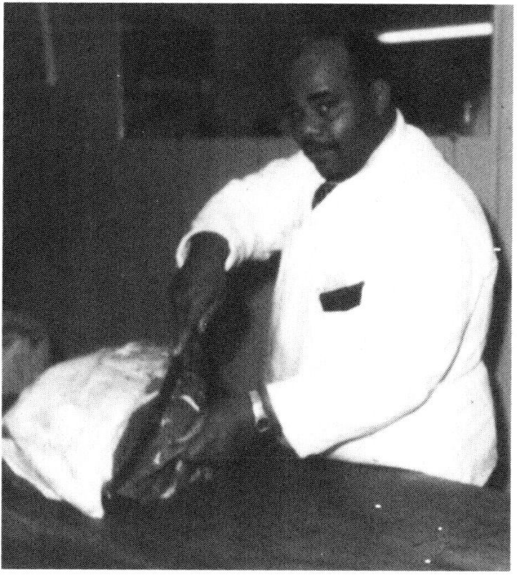

Lucien Campbell, seen working at Ren's Super Market, 2500 Home Avenue, became Dayton's first licensed black meatcutter in 1951. Courtesy of Lucien Campbell.

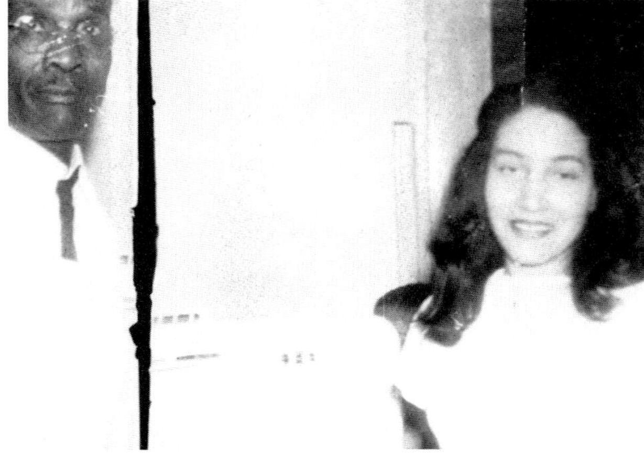

(Above Left)Henry Hollis, seen here with his daughter, Mrs. Anna Combs, came to Dayton from Kentucky in 1931. The family lived in North Dayton, off Valley Street, and then moved to Garst Street. Mr. Hollis worked at GH & R Foundry. (Black men who were restricted to the physically demanding, low-paying jobs said that GH & R meant "Go home and rest"). Mrs. Combs worked as a domestic and at Gallagher's Drugstore until she earned her license as a nurse. Courtesy of Deborah Combs.

(Above) Clarence Bowman Sr. founded the Bowman Funeral Chapel at 2060 Germantown in 1952. A member of Bethel Baptist Church and a past president of the local chapter of the NAACP, Bowman served on the board of trustees at Blue Cross of Southwestern Ohio, the Dayton Urban League, Good Samaritan Hospital, United Way, and the University of Dayton. The family now operates a second chapel at 3223 Hoover. Courtesy of the Bowman and Martin families.

(Left) Phillip Greer joined the Dayton police force in 1945 and was later promoted to detective. Other African Americans in the Dayton Police Department in 1951 included Lucious Gleaton, James B. Hogan, Diana Robinson, and Clifton Wilson. The small number of black officers—by the late 1960s fewer than six percent of the officers were black, and only one black officer was in a supervisory position in a city that was approximately thirty-two percent black—was a major issue in the African American community. Courtesy of Dan Blackburn.

After earning his Doctorate of Jurisprudence degree and graduating from Ohio State University in 1956, J. Paul Prear began his law practice and his involvement with the Republican Party. Paul and his brother Roger were major figures in the development and implementation of the program for Dayton's Model Cities Demonstration Project, which created jobs and was influential in the development of the Priority Board system. Courtesy of Jeanette Prear.

Russell Carter, the first black prosecutor and judge in Dayton, has helped bring about many changes. In 1948 he brought suit against the Biltmore Hotel, which would not allow Federal Judge William Hastie to register. Other hotels changed their policy. Carter was instrumental in Dr. Edward Bennett becoming the first black surgeon and Dr. Roger Taylor the first black intern at Miami Valley Hospital. Other lawyers practicing between 1941 and 1960 included Robert Bostick, J. B. Carter, T. C. Carter, Arthur Fisher, James McGee, Bush Mitchell, J. Paul Prear, and Morris Simmons. Courtesy of Russell L. Carter.

Truck driver Claude Bell was one of the many African Americans employed by the Dayton Malleable Iron Company at West Third and Summit Streets. Courtesy of Dan Blackburn.

(Above) Members of the Gem City Medical, Dental, and Pharmaceutical Society were among the guests at this party around 1958. Front row: Laura Jones, Rosamond Johnson, and Kathy Ford. Seated, second row: Virginia Seabrooks, Evangeline Donnelly, Naomi Haynes, Dr. and Mrs. Reginald Daniels, Maceola Taylor, Florence and Dr. Edward Bennett. Standing: Dr. Robert Ford, Celestine Cromartie, Dr. and Mrs. Stanley Earley, Dr. James E. Cromartie, Dr. Curtis Haynes, Dr. Lloyd Williams, Thelma Clarke, William Donnelly, Dr. Roger Taylor, Iva Coleman, Dr. Herbert Seabrooks, Dr. Maceo R. Clarke, William Jones, and Dr. Stanford Coleman. Other doctors included Lloyd Cox, J. Milton Dasher, Donald Gillim, Cecil Giscombe, Frederick Grigsby, James Gunn, Charles Johnson Jr., Owen McFall, Taylor Mealy, Jerome Miller, Gordon Munson, Russell Penman, George Pugh, Charles Rogers, B. A. Rose, W. Clifton Rowan, Lynn Taylor, and Edward Williams. Courtesy of Maceo R. Clarke, Jr.

Joe Davis (with daughter Delpha), his wife, Verchell, and her sister, Oshie, are shown at their home at 2814 Germantown. Davis came to Dayton from South Carolina in 1937 and began working as a short-order cook in the Greyhound terminal at Fourth and Wilkinson. After Albert Shropshire helped him get started in real estate, Davis bought three lots at Germantown and MacArthur. The Davises opened the first D & D Cleaners in 1945, and gave Johnny Wilder his first job. Verchell quit her job at Gentile (the Defense Electronics Supply Center) to work at their cleaning plant. By 1955 the Davises had four cleaning plants. Courtesy of Delpha Davis Moore.

(Left) Syble Hurt Anderson, the first African American in Miami Valley Hospital's nurses training program, graduated in 1954. She began working in Surgery and Recovery, and in 1957 was Head Nurse of All Night Surgery. Photograph by Robert Nehus Photos, courtesy of James Hurt and Vester Spears.

(Below) Bell's Drug Store, at 2228 Germantown, was founded by Shannon Bell, who came to Dayton in 1933. Seated in front of the store in the 1940s are Gerald Stroud, Bobby Lett, Eugene Taylor, Unidentified, Alvern Williams, and Leslie Hall. Photograph by Norman Stroud.

Lelia Francis, the first black realtor in Ohio, is seen leaving her office in the 1950s. Mrs. Francis fought against redlining and was arrested for demonstrating to force Rike-Kumler Department Store to hire black people. Her community activities have been recognized by many Dayton organizations, including the National Business League and the Greater Dayton Christian Council. In 1995, still involved and energetic at 91, Mrs. Francis continues to operate her real estate business at 507 South Summit Street. Collins Studio, courtesy of Lelia Francis.

(Left) John Henderson Sr. opened his first printing shop in his home on Kerney Street in 1941, and moved several times before opening the shop at 301 Washington. This shop is Dayton's oldest black-owned business east of the Miami River. Henderson, an all-around athlete at Wilberforce University, was an active member of Wayman Chapel A.M.E. Church, and of Equity Lodge No. 121, Amer Temple No. 107, Miami Consistory No. 26. Courtesy of the Henderson family.

(Below) Henderson's Printing continues as a family business in 1995. Shown are Eloise, John Jr., John Sr. (who died in 1991), Mrs. Mary Henderson, David, Marilyn, and Paul. Mrs. Henderson, a teacher, was selected as a Dayton Daily News *Top Ten Woman of 1977 for her community work, which included founding the Westwood Teenage Council in 1960. She began by taking into her home students who needed adult guidance and goals. In 1985, 125 members—including pastor Robert Goff, psychologist Valerie Bowling, teachers David, Eloise, and Marilyn Henderson, and WKEF-TV's Dale Richardson—held a reunion. Courtesy of the Henderson family.*

(Above) Mark Mayo Sr. (left) and his son Harry Sr., stand in front of the Mayo Skating Rink at 4623 Hoover Avenue. The Mayos, who opened the country's first black-owned skating rink at 1711 McCall in 1948, had a third rink at 4075 Germantown. The rinks became centers for black teens and their families. The McCall Street rink was closed in 1968; in 1969 Harry Jr. purchased the Germantown Street rink for his new Mayo Industries, which today has one hundred employees. The Hoover Skate Arena is still in operation, and skating at Mayo's is a three-generation tradition. Photo from Mainstream America, *courtesy of Harry Mayo Jr.*

(Left) In 1941 Edward Dugger, holder of the American record in the 120-yard high hurdles in 1940, became the first black engineer at Wright-Patterson Air Force Base. When Dugger retired in 1975, he was the Chief of the Scientific and Technical Information Division of the Materials Information Branch of the Materials Laboratory. Wright Patterson has been and continues to be a major employer of local African Americans. Courtesy of Mrs. Wertha Dugger-Smith.

(Below) The Dayton chapter of Alpha Phi Alpha fraternity was founded in 1921. Members in this 1970s photograph include, first row left to right: Otis Drake, Dr. G. S. Adebisi Adegbile, Rollison Barriteau, William Coleman, and Herman Anderson. Second row: George Findley, Michael Coleman, Robert Clarke, Charles Caldwell, James Washington, Eluster Fields, Joseph Collier, and Samuel Collier. Third row: James Tilton, Larry Carter, Fred Conway, Roy Taylor, John Long, Dr. Maceo Clarke, Unidentified, Larry Edwards, Leroy Edwards, Richard Allen, Leonard Raymond, and James Wright. Fourth row: Richard Hobson, Dwight Jackson, Wilbert Powell, Herman Dees, Grady Harris, Jake Brewer, Edward White, Thomas Bush, and Alonzo Connors. Top: James Adams, William Phylon, and Melvin Coleman. Members of the Dayton branch participate in Project Alpha, working with young men in grades 7–9. From the Luther White Collection, courtesy of the National Afro-American Museum and Cultural Center.

The Dayton Alumni Chapter of Kappa Alpha Psi fraternity was formed in November 1946, at the Fifth Street YMCA. The charter members included (seated) Lloyd Lewis Sr., R. A. Braxton, and Polemarch William McLoud, receiving the charter from Grand Board of Directors member Dr. Eugene Clark. Standing: Donald Dewitt, T. M. Zackary, William Quisenberry Jr., and Robert Penman. Polemarch McLoud established the Dayton branch of the Atlanta Life Insurance Company. Courtesy of Richard James.

In 1952 Mrs. Edith Hodge founded the Delta Phi Zeta Chapter of Zeta Phi Beta Sorority. She taught in the Dayton City Schools and in area universities for thirty-four years. In 1990 she gave Wilberforce University $60,000 to establish a scholarship fund in honor of her late husband, Dr. William Hodge, vice-chairman of the trustee board of Wilberforce University and presiding elder of the Third Episcopal District, A.M.E. Church. Courtesy of Mrs. Edith Hodge.

(Above) C. J. McLin Sr. (top) was one of those present at this Omega Psi Phi fraternity ball in the late 1940s. Others present included Mrs. McLin, Dr. and Mrs. Gunn (left of C.J.); Cal Crawford, second from the left in the second row, and his wife Evelyn, seated in front of him; and Lloyd Lewis Sr., fifth from the left in the second row, and his wife, Ruth, seated in front of him. Photograph by Chas. F. Morgan, courtesy of Lloyd Lewis Sr.

(Left) Camp 21 of the American Woodmen, a black-owned fraternal/insurance company, was organized in Dayton in 1915. Members in this 1950s photograph include, seated: (2) Hannah Garnett, Worthy Guardian, (5) Odessa Williams, and (6) Elizabeth Gibbs. Standing: (3) Wright Sumlin, (4) Supreme Commander Lawrence H. Lightner, (5) Mabel Williams, (6) Aaron Thomas, and (8) Vashti Owens. Photograph by Edwards Portable Studio, courtesy of Mabel Williams

The Dayton branch of the National Council of Negro Women (NCNW) was organized in 1957. The charter members are, front row left to right: Wanda Harris, Barbara King, Cathy Ford Bowman, Esther Carter, and Thelma Clarke. Middle row: Ella Lowry, Edna Earley, President Marianna Harris, Dr. Maureen Johnson, and Florence Bennett. Back row: Lorraine Poore, Lelia Francis, Marian Grigsby, Genevieve Douglas, Margaret Irby, Unidentified, Rosamond Johnson, Naomi Haynes, Freida Hairston, and Unidentified. NCNW, through programs such as the Black Family Reunion, perpetuates the work and legacy of its founder, Mary McLeod Bethune. Courtesy of Charity Adams Earley.

In 1957 Jack and Jill of America, Inc., raised more than one thousand dollars for the polio fund. The officers were Mildred Crumpton, president; Olivia Iles, vice president and teenage advisor; Rosamond Johnson, recording secretary; Mary Blackburn, corresponding secretary; Helen Washington, treasurer; June Marable, journalist; Wertha Dugger (pictured) chaplain; and Alice Montgomery, historian. Mothers and their children are the members of this service organization, which is dedicated to the interests of children. Brown Photos, courtesy of Wertha Dugger-Smith.

The Unique Study Club was formed in 1900. Members studied the works of black authors and participated in activities such as Emancipation Day parades, the women's suffrage movement, and other human rights struggles. The members in this 1960 photograph include, front: (2) Ida Forte and (3) Lilla Rogers. Middle row: (4) Grace Hampton, (5) Bertie Ellis, (9) Vashti Taylor, and (10) Adelaide Hand. Back row: (1) Margaret Irby, (3) Ella Lowry, (4) Nathanielle Bowman Martin, and (6) Marianna Harris. The club is still active in 1995. Courtesy of the Bowman and Martin families.

In 1948, members of Amer Temple #107 posed for this photograph at the DeSoto Bass Courts, near Clements. They included, front row: (1) Alexander Green, and (2) Harrison Martin. Back row: (1) J. C. Bowman, (2) Lawrence Bowman, (3) Elijah Kilborn, (5) Dr. Stanley Earley, (7) Ellis Bowers, and (10) Clarence Bowman. Courtesy of the Bowman and Martin families.

(Far Right) The Melissa Bess Day Care Center remained one of the many vital community/service organizations. Members of the Auxiliary Guild and the Board in this 1950s photograph include, front row: (1) Becky Shaw, (2) Laura Jones, (3) Reba Gaston, (4) Garnetta Fields Johns, and (5) Rosamond Johnson. Middle row: (2) Remitha Ford, (5) Melissa Bess, (6) Letitia Rose, (7) Agnes Shaw, and (8) Ruth Lewis. Back row: (2) Emily Tate, (3) Margaret Robinson, (4) Audrey Watson, (6) Naomi Haynes, (7) Rose Ellis, (8) Marie Stokes, and (11) Wilma Jackson. The center, at 1798 West Stewart, continues to serve the community in 1995. Photo by Furman Brown, courtesy of Rose Ellis.

On August 23, 1959, Dr. Charles H. Wesley, historian and past president of Central State University and Wilberforce University, delivered the oration at the cornerstone laying ceremony conducted by the Prince Hall Grand Lodge of Ohio. Grand Master Carl Wilson presided over the ceremony at the Prince Hall Masonic Temple, 2531 Germantown Street. From Wesley, History, *courtesy of the Prince Hall Grand Lodge of Ohio.*

In April 1942, the YWCA Board of Directors approved the purchase of the former residence of the Harry Kuhns family at 236 South Summit. The house (pictured) and the carriage house in the back were quickly remodeled, as there was a shortage of rooms due to segregation in housing. Fifty-six rooms were available at the Y, thirty in the house and twenty-six on the second floor of the former carriage house, known as the Barn. The Summit Street Y opened in October 1943, and closed in 1961. Courtesy of the Dayton YWCA.

In the 1950s, residents in the Mary Scott Home at 108 Garst Street, including Emma Starr (to the right of volunteer Marjorie Card) gather around the table. The home had to be moved in 1976 due to the construction of Edwin Moses Boulevard. It is now located at 3109 Campus Drive. Courtesy of the Mary Scott Nursing Center, Inc.

In the 1940s and 1950s, Mrs. Mamie G. Wilson, seen in front of her home at 120 Garst Street, served as a foster parent for many children being helped by the Montgomery County Children Services Bureau. Courtesy of Mrs. Wiletha McGuire, daughter.

(Right) The Summit Street YWCA benefited from the service of capable leaders such as Mattie Lyle, who served from 1952 through 1954. Mrs. Lyle was also active at Bethel Baptist Church, where she served in the church school for forty-one years. She was also a teacher in the Dayton Public Schools. Courtesy of the Dayton YWCA.

(Below) After Blonnie Jeter's family came to Dayton in 1929, Blonnie was helped by Mrs. John Rives, who hired her to deliver the Dayton Forum, *and by Mrs. Mabel Evens, who provided a membership at the YWCA. Later, Blonnie in turn helped others. In 1948 she organized Dayton's first black Camp Fire Girls unit. She also taught for the Montgomery County Board of Mental Retardation, and directed Camp Variety for the Handicapped. In 1968 Mrs. Jeter was honored by the* Dayton Daily News *as one of Dayton's Top Ten Women. Courtesy of Blonnie Jeter.*

(Above) Those who enjoyed using the facilities of the West Side YWCA in the early 1940s included, first row: (1) Pat Holcomb and (3) Anne Parsons. Second row: (2) Wanda Wheatley. Third row, second from the right, Becky Shaw. Fourth row: (2) Delores Miles. Last row, left end, Susannah Bass. Courtesy of the Dayton YWCA.

(Left) After coming to Dayton in 1947, Adelaide Hand met Lilla Rogers and Bertie Ellis, and became involved in the Unique Study Club and Linden Center. In 1994, one-hundred-year-old Mrs. Hand is still a member of the club and a volunteer at the center. Dayton has also benefited from the work of other senior citizens such as Richard Ellison, who helped form the Westwood Awareness Body. The Adelaide Hand Room at Linden Center and the Ellison Senior Citizen Center at 2412 West Dr. Martin Luther King Jr. Way, honor the contributions of Mrs. Hand and Mr. Ellison. Courtesy of the Dayton Art Institute.

Sports were an important leisure-time activity. Golf became more popular among African Americans after World War II. Seen in this 1948 photo are members of the Miami View Golf Club and the Golferettes. First row: Harold Johnson, Estella Williams, and Curtis Lloyd. Second row: Grace Cunningham, Evelyn Watkins, Grace Grubbs, Lula Henderson, Flora Delaney, Martha Ferguson, Myrtice McIver, and Eva Garrett. Third row: Edgar Nickerson, George Gibbs, Norman Coleman, Laura Jones, Willie Bowling, Ora Kelley, and John Card. Fourth row: Clarence Smith, Wilcher Morton, Robert Nelson, Edna Riffe (1944 Lady Amateur Champion), Eunice Lee, Edrias Stinson, Viola Lloyd, Robert Kelley, and James Lee. Fifth row: George Williams, Joe Riffe, Myron Coleman, Glenn Patterson, Mose Gustius, Bruce Highwarden, Ovil Goins, Leonard Stevenson, Ike Delaney, and Jule Yoter. An Austin photo, courtesy of Viola Riffe Lloyd.

(Right) In 1944 - 45, Daytonians enjoyed watching the semiprofessional Dayton Bombers, three of whom are seen practicing at DeSoto Bass Courts. George Vaughn recalls that the team's sponsors were Pop Mason and Harry Lightfoot. Players included Tommy Austin and Edward "Snag" Rice. "Cool Papa" Turley was the coach. The Bombers played teams such as Kentucky State College. Photograph by Norman Stroud.

Lewis E. Logan Jr., seen after knocking down his opponent in the 1946 Dayton Golden Gloves competition, won forty-eight straight bouts as a member of St. John's Boxing Program. He was a member of Dave Albritton's championship boxing team at Dunbar, and a Golden Gloves champion in 1946, 1947, and 1948. Logan helped Sugar Ray Robinson train for his title fight with Tommy Bell and was inducted into Dayton's Boxing Hall of Fame in 1980. Lewis, the son of pioneer grocer Reverend L. E. Logan Sr., and the brother of hotel/restaurant owner Ben Logan, continues the family tradition of entrepreneurship and community service as the owner of Zach's Seafood at Groveland and Germantown. Army photo by Post Signal Photo Lab, Fort Hood, Texas. Courtesy of Lewis E. Logan, Jr.

Included in this 1950s photograph of the Stokes Question Marks softball team are, front row: Anne Hart, Helen Reese, Debbie Brown, and Mary Ann Fields. Back row: Oney Ross, Unidentified, Julia Carr, Lavinia Kelly, Annie Stokes, Honey, Coach Charles Stokes, and Pauline Saunders. In 1994 Stokes was inducted into Dayton's Women's Fast Pitch Hall of Fame. She and Charles, inducted into Dayton's Basketball Hall of Fame in 1975, are the only husband/wife team so honored. Courtesy of Charles Stokes.

(Far Left) Daytonians also enjoyed spending time at C. J. McLin's Farm Dell on Ruth Avenue. Seen in this 1940s photograph are Cosmopolitan Club members (3) Charlie Bryant, (4) Andre Fletcher, (5) Eugene Taylor, (6) Oscar Pettiford, (8) Roger Murphy, (9) Tillman McGuire, and (10) Roy Shaw. The Cosmopolitan Club was a social club, whose members got together for fun and relaxation. Photograph by Norman Stroud.

After walking from 246 Homestead Avenue, author Margaret Peters (holding Wendell), her other brothers, Andrew (left) and Joseph, and her sister, Rosemary, enjoyed an outing at Burkham Park on Broadway in 1947. The park provided recreation for those living in Edgemont and the surrounding area. Courtesy of the Peters family.

(Above) In the 1950s, these Cub Scouts at St. James Catholic Church in Edgemont posed with their adviser, Mrs. Perkins. Courtesy of the Archdiocese of Cincinnati and St. James Catholic Church.

(Left) In 1955, Karen and Sandra Blanchard enjoyed riding the carousel at Lakeside Park at Lakeview and Gettysburg. Courtesy of Chester Blanchard.

(Above) In 1957, the Grandmothers Club held this outing at McCabe Park. The club, organized in the early 1950s, arranged activities such as picnics and masquerade parties. Photograph by Edward Taylor.

(Right) The girls who graduated from St. John Catholic School in 1942 posed with Father Tessing. Front row: Emma (Fisher) Adkins, and Yvonne Lewis. Middle: Lucille Fant, Lulu (Warnock) Jackson, and Bonnie Davis. Back: Mattie Jordan, Alberta Cain, Georgiana Henry, Vivian Thomas, and Lois Bridges. Courtesy of Lulu Warnock Jackson.

(Left) Jessie Hathcock, seen with Esther Carter (left) and Judy Poore in this 1950s photograph, was representative of the excellence of Dunbar's staff. She was the first black woman to graduate from the University of Dayton, a founder of the Women's Christian Association (WCA) No. 2, the first president of Beta Eta Omega Chapter of Alpha Kappa Alpha Sorority, Inc., chairman of the Dayton branch of the National Association of College Women, and an outspoken foe of racism. She introduced many students to Paul Laurence Dunbar's writings, and brought in speakers such as Dr. W. E. B. Du Bois. Courtesy of the Dayton Daily News.

(Below) In 1957, Dunbar High School's staff included, back row: William Garland, Jack Waller, Principal Lloyd Phillips, Leo Stewart, Jack Hart, Robert Rice, William Harrison, William Scott, Theodore Wiley, Ivory Suseberry, Bill Edwards, and David Williams. Middle row: Luther White, James Ross Jr., William Woods, Marie Stokes, Jessie Hathcock, Tecora Neil, Evelyn Jackson, Susana Ross, William Young, Grace Parker, Sam Ewing, Richard Payne, Emerson Harewood, and Clarens Francois. Front row: Ruth Richardson, student teacher, Ada Barriteau, Tommie Tucker, Marguerite Turner, Geneva Turpin, Martha Gunn, Elizabeth Wright, Laura Jones, Vivian Kalfus, Madelyn Cisco, Bernice Sumlin, and Annabelle Carter. Photograph by Robert Knoll Studio, courtesy of James Ross Jr.

The 1948–49 city champions in basketball were Dunbar Wolverines Sage Brown, Azariah Smith, Oscar Dominick, Arthur Dukes, Henry Macbeth, William Reid, Curtis Oldham, John Jackson, Leonard Macbeth, David Jones, John Sherrer, Jimmy Wright, Bob Hoskins, William Rakestraw, and Harold Jackson. Like Dave Albritton, basketball coach Luther White and football coaches Stanglaws Slater and Jack Hart stressed education and character, as well as athletics. Courtesy of Robert Knoll Studio.

In 1948–49 Dunbar won city championships in track, basketball, and cross country. Members of the track team, which also won the state championship, posed with their coach, David Albritton, a silver medal winner in the 1936 Olympics. Top: Lavern Taylor. Kneeling: Vernon Stroud, Elijah Crane, Jonathan Bass, Maceo Cofield, and Frank Kilgore. Albritton led two more track teams to state titles and had a positive influence on many young men, including future mayor Richard Clay Dixon. Albritton also served the Dayton community as a member of the Ohio House of Representatives (1960–64), and as the owner of an insurance company. Albritton died in 1994. Courtesy of Robert Knoll Studio.

Dunbar 1959 graduate M. C. McGuire, who played for the Baltimore Orioles in 1962 and 1967, is seen here during his senior year, when he played with the Dorothy Lane Market team. Other Dayton Public School graduates who became professional athletes include Martin Bayless (Belmont), James Caldwell, Drake Garrett, Larry Lee, and Dan Wilkinson (Dunbar), Ron Harper (Kiser), Marco Coleman (Patterson), Leo Hayden (Roosevelt), Keith Byars (Roth), and Doug France, (Colonel White). Courtesy of M. C. McGuire.

The Roosevelt High School Teddies won the state basketball championship in 1954. Shown are, front: managers Ronnie Thompson and Chuck Hildreth. Second row: Reserve coach Leo Kelley, Tom Armstrong, Jerry Morgan, Norman Lee, Willie Donaldson, Bill Gleason, Steve Vegso, Bob Reed, and freshman coach Dave Gorby. Last row: Coach John Woolums, Dave Walters, Bill Barker, Anthony Steele, Jim Zolman, Bob Cyphers, Uriah Hollis, Joe McCloud, and faculty manager Loren Zimmerman. After graduating, Norman Lee played with the Harlem Globetrotters for ten years. Courtesy of the Dayton Daily News.

In 1960 Roosevelt High School again won the state basketball championship. Shown are, front row: Henry Burlong, L. C. Snow, James Boyd, Ray Brown, Buford Davis, John Henderson, Joe Shaw, and mascot Troddy Beery. Back row: Coach John Woolums, Eugene Van Hoose, John Shehee, Tommy Lewis, James Terry, Horace Gaulding, reserve coach Leo Kelley, and freshman coach Gene Cultice. After graduating from the University of Michigan, Henderson played football for the Detroit Lions for one year, and then for the Minnesota Vikings until 1973. After retiring, he became an employee relations executive for Honeywell. Courtesy of the Dayton Daily News.

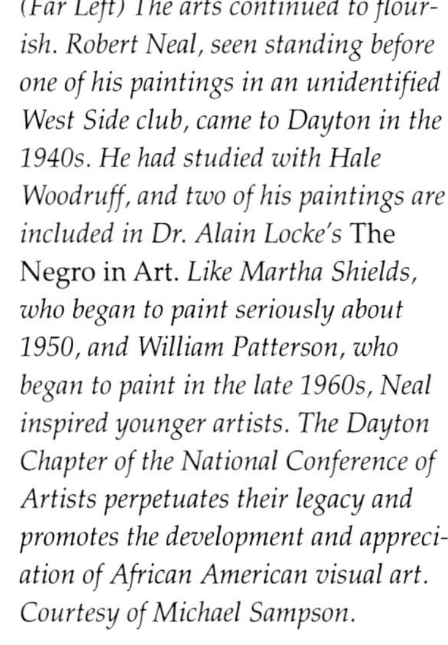

(Far Left) The arts continued to flourish. Robert Neal, seen standing before one of his paintings in an unidentified West Side club, came to Dayton in the 1940s. He had studied with Hale Woodruff, and two of his paintings are included in Dr. Alain Locke's The Negro in Art. *Like Martha Shields, who began to paint seriously about 1950, and William Patterson, who began to paint in the late 1960s, Neal inspired younger artists. The Dayton Chapter of the National Conference of Artists perpetuates their legacy and promotes the development and appreciation of African American visual art. Courtesy of Michael Sampson.*

(Left) The Stars of Joy were the first local black group to sing gospel on WHIO radio. The members in this 1950 photograph are, seated: James Selmon and Lonzo Wilks. Standing: James Banks, Roosevelt Williams (one of the first black men to pour steel at Harris Seybold on Washington Street), Robert Lorne, and James Hunter. Courtesy of daughter Darlene Williams Evans.

Willis "Bing" Davis, whose family was part of the African American community in East Dayton, was All-City in basketball and track at Wilbur Wright High School, where Archie Lewis was admired because he had used his athletic ability to obtain a college education. After graduating from DePauw University, Bing taught art at Colonel White High School (overcoming opposition to his placement at the then predominantly white school) the Living Arts Center, and DePauw and Wright State Universities. In 1978 he became chair of Central State University's Art Department. Bing has won international recognition for his work. Courtesy of Bing Davis.

(Above) Artist Kathleen Patterson (right) and her husband, Postell Patterson (seated), seen here with their nephew Dr. Frederick Patterson and Mrs. Russell McCalla at Carillon Historical Park, came to Dayton in 1956. Mrs. Patterson is a member of the Dayton Society of Painters. Postell helped Carillon acquire a buggy made by the Pattersons, the only black company that manufactured an automobile. Mrs. McCalla is the former owner of the buggy. Courtesy of Kathleen Patterson.

(Far Right) Barbara-O, seen here at age four in her grandmother's yard on Dennison, began acting when she was eleven years old. Her credits include Freedom Road *with Muhammad Ali and the highly acclaimed* Daughters of the Dust. *Other local performers who have achieved fame outside of Dayton include Dorian Harewood, Donna Wood, and Bruce Davis. Davis, who appeared in* All That Jazz, *attributes much of his success to Clarence Young III, director of Theater West and author of* Perry Mission, *which was performed in New York in 1971 by the Negro Ensemble Company. Courtesy of Barbara-O.*

Enjoy a journey into the past as you recall many of the West Fifth Street/ Germantown area establishments which existed between the 1870's & the 1950's.

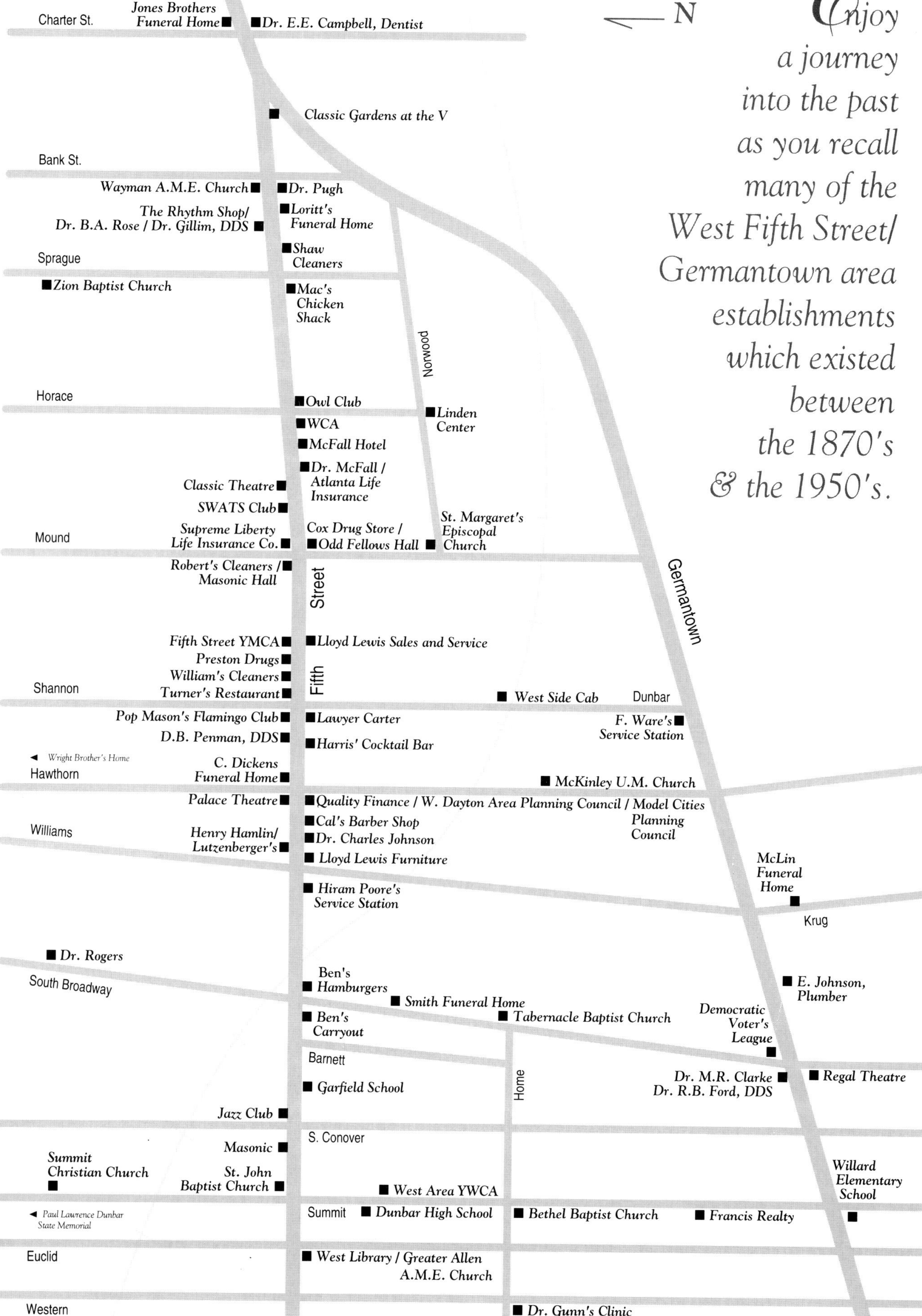

Fifth Street

By 1940, segregated housing patterns had resulted in eighty-four percent of Dayton's African American population being concentrated on the West Side. That area experienced a tremendous growth in businesses, professional offices, and entertainment centers. On West Fifth Street, between Bank and Broadway, the number of these establishments increased from forty-three in 1920 to seventy-one in 1940. (Mitchell, *The Mound-Horace Area*)

Fifth Street became the center of black life. After going to church on Sunday, many residents went to the Classic or the Palace, and then to Cox's drugstore for the best ice cream soda in Dayton. Gaynelle Ward, ticket-taker at the Classic in 1953 and 1954, remembers watching well-dressed black people "strolling" on Fifth Street. There were Midnight Rambles at the Palace, good meals at the YMCA, and good times at Harris' Cocktail Bar.

Music was an important part of life on Fifth Street, and Dayton both produced and attracted great entertainers.

This map, which shows some of the businesses and other establishments in the Fifth Street/Germantown Street area, was drawn by State Representative Lloyd Lewis Jr. The graphic design was done by Renee Sallee, Creative Director of Sallee Design.

In 1923, after the Keith Theater opened at Fourth and Ludlow, black Daytonians were barred from downtown theaters. Responding to this discrimination, entrepreneurs Carl Anderson (pictured) and Giles Goodrich built the Classic Theater in 1926. Carl was a gracious owner, who gave his employees bonus checks and Christmas dinners at the YMCA. When he died in 1939, more than 2,000 people came to St. Margaret's Episcopal Church to pay their respects. Courtesy of the Montgomery County Historical Society.

The Classic, with its marble lobby and beautiful ballroom, opened on August 25, 1926. Bessie Ward was the organist. Black students from Roosevelt, who organized their own activities because of the discrimination at the high school, held their own prom in the ballroom in 1940. Courtesy of the Montgomery County Historical Society.

SATURDAY, OCTOBER 29

—Double Feature Program—

—Feature No. 1—

—Feature No. 2—

—Added—

Selected Short Subjects

402—National Program & Printing Co.

SUNDAY Through FRIDAY
OCTOBER 30 Through NOVEMBER 4
6 — Big Days — 6
Big Double Feature Program

THE GREAT NEGRO ACTOR
PAUL ROBESON
In His Most Memorable Role
"THE SONG OF FREEDOM"
With an All Colored Cast

ELISABETH WELCH
GEORGE MOZART
ESME PERCY
JOAN FRED EMMEY
ARTHUR WILLIAMS
RONALD SIMPSON
JENNY DEAN
BERNARD ANSELL
ROBERT ADAMS
CORNELIA SMITH
SYDNEY BENSON
WILL HAMMER
ALF GODDARD
AMBROSE MANNING

Also PHYLLIS BROOKS and RICARDO CORTEZ in
"CITY GIRL"
There's Also
Selected Short Subjects

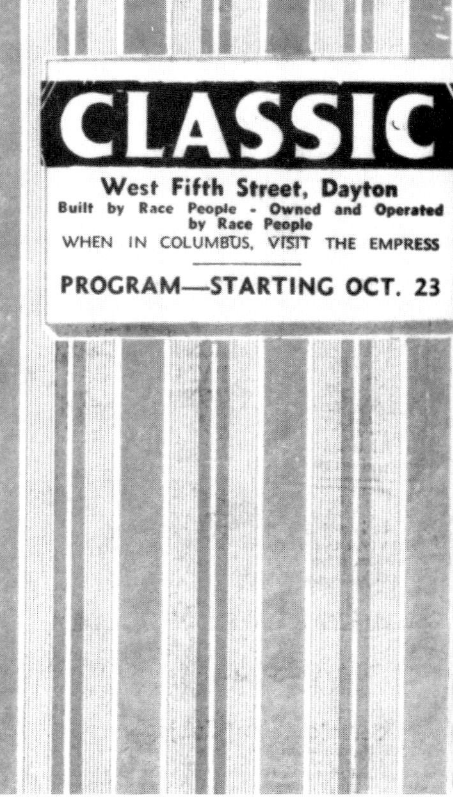

CLASSIC
West Fifth Street, Dayton
Built by Race People - Owned and Operated by Race People
WHEN IN COLUMBUS, VISIT THE EMPRESS
PROGRAM—STARTING OCT. 23

(Above) The Classic generally showed three different programs each week. However, special features such as the Paul Robeson film advertised on this 1939 playbill had longer runs. In the 1940s children could see a double feature, a serial, a newsreel, and a cartoon for sixteen cents. Movies of Joe Louis's fights were very popular. The front side of the playbill also shows how Carl Anderson sought to promote pride and the patronizing of black businesses. Courtesy of Everett Bruce.

(Far Left) Everett Bruce, seen in his uniform in front of the Classic, was an usher from 1937 through 1939. Courtesy of Everett Bruce.

(Above) In 1927, the West Side Amusement Corporation, with Valentine Winters as president and Dr. Lloyd Cox as vice president, began constructing the Westside Community Center at Fifth and Williams Streets. It included the Palace Theater, a drugstore, and a ballroom known as the Cotton Club. Courtesy of the Montgomery County Historical Society.

(Right) The Classic also offered live entertainment. Jennie Swann, whose father, Anderson Mumford, owned Mumford Dry Cleaners across from the Classic, remembers seeing Lena Horne and Piqua's Mills Brothers (pictured) at the Classic. Courtesy of George Banks.

(Far Right) Ella Fitzgerald appeared at the Cotton Club, the ballroom above the Palace, on November 23, 1939. She was one of many top performers, such as Count Basie and Billy Eckstine, brought to the Cotton Club by Elwood Parsons' and Earl Preston Taylor's Paramount Amusement Club. Parsons was also the first black baseball scout in the major leagues. Courtesy of the Dayton Daily News.

Seen playing at the Crystal Lounge in the 1940s are (1) Malcolm Taylor, (3) bandleader Prince Davis, and (6) Phillip Wright. Davis, who studied with Clarens Francois at Dunbar High School, met Duke Ellington and other stars while delivering placards for the Paramount Amusement Club. During World War II, he played in the Navy band. Davis continues to play, often with long-time favorites Roy Edge and Don Sutton. Courtesy of Prince Davis.

Dunbar High School teacher Bill Young, the trumpet player on the right, also led his own band in the late thirties and early forties. The drummer was John Pitman; the singer was Mary Floyd. Courtesy of Prince Davis.

(Above) Buddy Webb, seen here as a member of the Navy band at the Great Lakes Naval Training Station during World War II, was one of the many great musicians of this era. Later Buddy led his own big band, which included Jimmy Thompson, Don Young, Clifford Crutcher, and Malcolm Taylor. Courtesy of Mrs. Irene Webb.

(Left) Mitchell "Booty" Wood (third from the right), a Dunbar High School graduate who had studied with music teacher Clarens Francois, began playing in West Side jazz clubs. In 1941 he joined Lionel Hampton's band at the Apollo Theater. He later played with Count Basie and Duke Ellington. Wood often returned to Dayton and played with his own band. Shown with him in this 1950s photograph of his local band are Raymond Herring, Bob Sampson, Chuck Breece (road manager), Edward Rice, Clarence Hall, Tezo Miller (who played with Ray Charles), and Roosevelt High School graduate Malcolm Taylor (who played with Duke Ellington, Illinois Jacquet, and Dizzy Gillespie). Courtesy of Bob Sampson.

(Left) Trumpeter Eugene "Snooky" Young, seen here with Johnny Carson and Skitch Henderson on "The Tonight Show," studied with Clarens Francois at Dunbar High School. He joined Jimmie Lunceford's band in 1939 and later played with Lionel Hampton and Count Basie. In 1962, he joined the NBC Orchestra. On September 9, 1989, Snooky returned to Dayton to headline CityFolk's Jazz Tradition concerts. Mayor Richard Clay Dixon proclaimed that day "Snooky Young Day." Courtesy of the Dayton Daily News.

(Above Left) Lester Bass, another student of Clarens Francois, calls "Booty" Wood his mentor. When Wood left Hampton's band, he recommended Bass for his chair, and Bass's career took off. Like other musicians, Bass returned to Dayton in the 1950s as the popularity of the big bands declined. He played at clubs such as the Farm Dell and worked at GH & R Foundry during the day. Bass also played with Snooky Young and the Roy Meriwether Trio. Courtesy of the Dayton Daily News.

(Above Right) Roy Meriwether began playing the piano when he was three. He accompanied the choir in his father's church—First Baptist Church in West Carrollton, which was moved to Dayton and renamed First Thessalonians Missionary Baptist Church—and performed with gospel singers. This gospel/blues influence was evident when he began playing jazz in the late 1950s. Roy is also a composer. His twenty-one-piece suite Black Snow *traces the history of the African American experience in the United States. Roy lives in New York City and continues to record, to tour, and to compose. Courtesy of the* Dayton Daily News.

Johnny Lytle, whom Lionel Hampton called "the greatest vibes player on the scene today" in 1960 (Shelton, "Springfield"), is from Springfield, Ohio, but he has long been part of Dayton's music scene. In 1960, while playing in the area, he stopped at George Tuck's Lavender Lounge and heard Bobbie Gordon singing. He was so impressed that he helped her get more engagements. They have been friends ever since. Courtesy of the Dayton Daily News.

(Right) Bobbie Gordon (Nell Brookshire) came to Dayton from Mississippi in 1945. She began singing at Wogaman Elementary School and at Mt. Enon Missionary Baptist Church. From 1962 through 1967, she sang at the Cascades at the invitation of Leroy Rogers. In 1970, while Bobbie was traveling with her own band, Booty Wood and Malcolm Taylor introduced her to Mercer Ellington, who introduced her to his father. In 1971, she was on the cover of Jet, *which did a five-page story about Duke's beautiful new vocalist. Now back in Dayton, Bobbie still enjoys going to Mt. Enon and singing. Courtesy of Bobbie Gordon.*

(Left) Many other local musicians, such as Billy Strayhorn and Chuck Connors, became nationally and internationally known. However, Cliff Bailey, one of the area's most popular and most influential musicians, laughingly admitted that he never made it big. Bailey, seen in the audience during one of his Sacred Concerts at Zion Baptist Church, performed in the Dayton area from 1955 until 1985, and served as an officer in the musicians' union (AFM Local 101-473). Bailey died in 1991, but members of his old band continue to play as New Traditions. Courtesy of Zion Baptist Church.

The Waiters and Bellman Club at 1333 West Fifth Street was owned by Wardell Griffin (left end). Others in this 1949 photograph include (3) Kid Malone, (4) Charles Lumpkin, and (7) Marian Brown. The performers are left-handed guitarist Peanut, vocalist Boddie, pianist/bandleader Count Lionel (and his new piano "Hedy Lamarr"), and bass player Elwood Berry. The club was known for its entertainment, its Thursday night Talent Show, and its food prepared by Big Ella McDay. Courtesy of Wardell Griffin.

Harry Lightfoot's Record Shop at 1017 West Fifth was one of Dayton's first black-owned record shops. Standing in front of the shop in the 1940s are Irvin Lewis, Dick Manuel, Harry Lightfoot Jr., Charles "Conk" Good, and Clarence Harris. Photograph by Norman Stroud.

(Left) Lloyd Lewis Sr. opened this service station at 918 West Fifth in 1937. It had a Service Department that cleaned spark plugs for five cents, an Auto Sales Department, and a Household Appliances Department. Lewis, the sponsor of WHIO Radio's Negro Business Hour hosted by Arthur Fisher, owned the station until 1969 when it was purchased by the city as part of an urban renewal plan. The building was razed in 1980. Photograph by Arnett Bates, courtesy of Lloyd Lewis Sr.

(Above) James H. McGee was one of the many African American professionals whose offices were on West Fifth Street. In the 1950s McGee earned a reputation as a militant lawyer due to the many civil rights suits he filed on behalf of the NAACP to end discrimination in restaurants and other public facilities. In 1970 he became Dayton's first black mayor. In 1988 Western Avenue was renamed James H. McGee Boulevard. Courtesy of James H. McGee.

(Right) During World War II, Jimmy Wilkerson, Mary Crews (Wonders), and Otis Phillips paused in their stroll along Fifth Street to pose for this photograph. Wilkerson was the first black class president at the University of Dayton, Mary (and Solomon Caulker from Sierra Leone) founded the Co-Ed Club, and Otis was an expert presser at Williams Dry Cleaners on Fifth Street. Photograph by Norman Stroud.

LeRoy Cox opened his drugstore at Fifth and Mound in 1920, and provided both fountain and pharmaceutical services. The latter were helpful to the sixteen black doctors with offices on West Fifth Street between 1921 and 1960. They were Doctors Adolphus Biggs, James Bush, Emmett Campbell, Sanders Coston, Lloyd Cox, Donald Gillim, Lloyd Hathcock, Charles Johnson, Owen McFall, Russell Penman, George Pugh, Thomas Robinson, B. Andrew Rose, W. Clifton Rowan, and Lynn Taylor. Courtesy of Grace Bailey.

The SWATS Club at 825 West Fifth was a favorite eating place. This group included (1) Harrison Sanders, (2) Jimmy Jones, (3) Lester Fish, (4) Buddy Evans, (5) Juddie Fisher, (7) Marjorie McGregor (hand on chin), the first black person to serve as president of the Board of Directors of the Dayton YWCA, (9) Nelson O'Neal, and (10) Roberta O'Neal. Courtesy of Mrs. Lewis McGregor.

The YMCA's Big Ten Team poses with John Green, who was executive secretary of the Y from 1929 until 1946. Seated are Charles Stokes, Johnny Arnold, Oscar Kimbrough, J. Paul Prear, and Sterling Brown. Standing are John Green, James Stone, Edward Rice, Tunney Fisher, Talmadge McKinney, Daniel Goins, Robert Prear, and Coach John Copeland. The Y also served as a restaurant (in 1923 blacks were barred from all downtown restaurants except Moses Moore's, Union Station, and the bus station), and provided dormitories, meeting rooms, a gym, and a swimming pool. Courtesy of Charles Stokes.

The Classic closed in 1959 as television and the end of segregation took their toll. Despite efforts to save the building, it was demolished in 1991. Courtesy of the Montgomery County Historical Society.

(Above) This is the three-level interchange for I-75 and 4, "in the heart of the city," looking north from I-75. Cutting into the heart of Dayton had a devastating effect on many neighborhoods, including West Fifth Street. Photograph from the Public Information Bureau, Ohio Department of Highways, July 10, 1961. Courtesy of the Dayton and Montgomery County Public Library.

(Right) Garfield Jones moved his funeral home to this building at 455 West Fifth Street in 1927, eighteen years after opening his business at 425 West Fifth. He remained on West Fifth for fifty-five years, until the construction of I-75 forced him to relocate in 1963. He moved to 2060 Germantown. For many older Daytonians, his moving symbolized the end of the West Fifth Street era. However, the memories of Fifth Street and other neighborhoods remain, and inspire Daytonians to work to solve today's problems. Photograph by Edward Taylor, courtesy of the Jones family.

(Above) Loretta Chandler directs the Children's Choir at Central Missionary Baptist Church, which was founded in 1966. Other churches founded during the 1960s include Antioch, Canaan, Christian, and True Vine Missionary Baptist; Greater Damascus, Mt. Carmel, Mt. Moriah, and United Baptist; and Christ Holy Temple. Courtesy of Reverend Raleigh Trammell.

(Far Right) In 1961, Don Crawford became the first black person elected to the Dayton City Commission. In 1967, he became the commission clerk and served in that position until 1990. When he retired, Mayor Richard Clay Dixon noted that Crawford was the last of the group of pioneers that included Arthur O. Fisher, James H. McGee, and C. J. McLin Jr. Crawford cautioned black Daytonians not to become complacent because the city had its second black mayor and numerous blacks in top administrative positions, and warned that the challenges of the future might be greater than avoiding the riots of the 1960s. Courtesy of Don Crawford.

Chapter Six

From the 1960s into the Twenty-First Century

From the 1960s into the 1990s, each decade brought new challenges to African Americans in Dayton. During the 1960s, Dayton's black population increased from 57,288 to 74,284. However, for the first time, Dayton's total population decreased from 262,332 to 242,917 as "white flight" occurred. WDAO, the first FM station in the United States with a black, urban format, began broadcasting. Reverend Henry Parker of Shiloh Baptist Church, who still bears scars from cattle prods, was among the Daytonians who fought for civil rights in the South. Dayton, like other urban areas, was hit by civil unrest. West Dayton bore the brunt of that upheaval. In 1966, a one-day "riot" occurred after the murder of Lester Mitchell by a group of white men ignited anger that had been growing during years of discrimination. The National Guard was called in. Many of the burned-out businesses were not rebuilt, so black Daytonians had to shop outside the community. The job market continued to change. For the first time, professional, technical, and kindred workers was one of the top five categories for both male and female black workers. The second highest category for both groups was service workers, except private household.

The 1970s

During the 1970s, Dayton's total population continued to decline, dropping from 242,917 to 193,444. The black population increased only from 74,284 to 75,016, as some of the more affluent black people moved to the suburbs. Dayton continued to produce top musicians, and nine bands secured national recording contracts. Dayton played a combination of disco and rock, with gospel and rhythm and blues (R & B) influences.

Faze-O recorded "Breakin' the Funk." Heatwave's "Too Hot to Handle" sold ten million copies. Lakeside's "All the Way Live" reached number five on *Billboard's* R & B charts. The Ohio Players' "Skin Tight" topped both the pop and the R & B charts. Platypus toured with the O'Jays. Shadow recorded "Love Lite." Slave's "Slave" and Sun's "Sunburn" went gold. (Lipper, "Sound")

School desegregation was a controversial topic. In 1972 the NAACP brought suit, charging the Dayton School Board with having created a deliberate pattern of segregation. After many court battles and the murder of desegregation expert Dr. Charles Glatt by segregationist Neal Long, busing for desegregation began. The top employment category was service workers. However, the second category was administrative support, including clerical, indicating another change in the job market.

Almost 58,000 Americans—twenty-three percent of whom were African Americans—lost their lives in the Vietnam War, the most divisive war for Americans since the Civil War. Daytonian Charles Redd Jr., shown in Dong Ha just after coming in off patrol, served three tours of duty in Vietnam: 1966, 1967, and part of 1969. Because of the morally ambiguous nature of the war, he and others who served did not receive the honor accorded those who had served in earlier wars. Finally in 1986, when the Vietnam Veterans Memorial Park of the Greater Dayton Area was dedicated, Daytonians honored the patriotism and sacrifice of all who had served, including the 412 who died or who were declared missing in action. Courtesy of Charles Redd Jr.

The 1980s

During the 1980s, Dayton's total population continued to decline, dropping from 193,444 to 182,044. For the first time, the black population also declined, dropping from 75,016 to 73,595 as Dayton, like many other cities, suffered from suburbanization and the loss of industry. Edison Elementary School was selected as a National School of Excellence. The first Dayton Black Cultural Festival was held in 1982. Christ Redeemer African Methodist Episcopal; Glory Tabernacle, New Faith and Spirit of Faith Missionary Baptist; and Second Thessalonians Baptist Churches were begun during this decade. Racial tension continued. In 1983 Tyree Broomfield became Dayton's first black police chief. Many members of the Fraternal Order of Police (FOP) resented Broomfield's appointment, and he had a troubled tenure. In 1989, four black police officers and a group of black ministers brought suit against the city and the FOP, claiming that a ten percent black police force in a forty percent black city was unjust. The top occupations were service, administrative support, and machine operators. Laborers were only a part of the seventh category—handlers, equipment cleaners, helpers, and laborers. Black Daytonians would have to prepare to compete in a changing job market.

C. J. McLin Jr., a superb organizer, could mobilize voters. He played a key role in Don Crawford's election to the city commission in 1961. Elected to the Ohio House of Representatives in 1966, McLin served for eleven terms. He exerted an influence at the national level, and co-chaired Jesse Jackson's 1958 presidential campaign. McLin played a leading role in the passage of many bills, including those that enabled Dayton to annex the airport, provided an extra state subsidy for Central State University, and established both the National Afro-American Museum and Cultural Center in Wilberforce, and the medical school at Wright State University. Courtesy of the National Afro-American Museum and Cultural Center.

(Above) The Roth High School Falcons were the city basketball champions for 1969–70. Shown are Dwight Kirk, Mike John, Bobby Oldham, Donald Smith, William Shotwell, James Allen, Henry McBeth, Larry Hamrick, Michael White, Loveless Crayton, Darrell Brice, Phillip Lumpkin, Delbert Render, Robert Hinesman, and coach Paul Palumbo. Smith—All-City, All-State, and All-American—was the leading scorer in the Dayton Public School League with a total of 1,336 points. Photograph by Robert Knoll Studios, courtesy of Donald Smith.

(Far Left) Dr. Abdul Alim Muhammad, the spokesperson for Minister Louis Farrakhan and an outstanding leader in the field of HIV/AIDS research, became a member of the Nation of Islam in 1968 while he was living in Dayton and studying at Antioch College. That year Dr. Muhammad, a civil rights/antiwar activist who had participated in the march on Washington and the 1966 march in Chicago, bought a copy of Muhammad Speaks at Westown. Attacted to the Nation of Islam by its emphasis on building both character and institutions, he joined Mosque No. 19. Dr. Muhammad established his Abundant Life Clinic in Washington, D.C. in 1986. For the past three years he has concentrated on HIV/AIDS research. Photograph by Francis Butler, Baltimore, Maryland. Courtesy of Dr. Abdul Alim Muhammad.

The internationally honored Dayton Contemporary Dance Company (DCDC) evolved from classes Jeraldyne Blunden began teaching at Linden Center in 1968. Shown in the front row are Nancy Arnold, Carol Ann Kilborn, Melanie Francis, and Sheila Hall. Middle row: Barbara Webb, Kathleen Maxey, Harvina Fisher, Jo Anna White, and Helen Parsons. Back row: Jeraldyne Blunden, Nancy Thomas, Shirley Caldwell, Lynette Shaw, and Sylvia Nelson. Photograph by the Dayton Daily News, courtesy of the Dayton Contemporary Dance Company.

(Above) The Links, Incorporated, work in four program areas: national trends and services, international trends and services, services to youth, and the arts. In 1973 the Dayton chapter presented Ed Bradley to a capacity crowd at the University of Dayton's Kennedy Union. Members of the Dayton chapter included, front row: Odessa Johnson, Odessa Robinson, Mrs. Taylor, Carolyn Fisher, Elizabeth Stratton, and Hortense Campbell. Second row: Billye Dasher, Ruth Lewis, Martha Gunn, Remitha Ford, Rosamond Johnson, and Vashti Taylor. Third row: Audrey Parker, Margaret Robinson, Violet Finley, and Dixie Wood. Top: Edythe Lewis and Hattie Wills. Courtesy of Gladys Gunn.

(Right) Dr. Lewis A. Jackson, aviation pioneer and developer of the NAV-KIT aircraft computer, served as the fourth president of Central State University before he became vice president for administration at Sinclair Community College in 1973. He fostered an entrepreneurial program so students at Sinclair could see themselves as employers. Courtesy of Dr. Violet Jackson.

The Colonel White High School Lady Cougars were the city champions in 1976–77. Shown in the front row: Shelle Johnson, Tammy Stritenberger, Paula Smith, Jeannie Hindsman, Michelle Middlebrook, Sonya Ray, manager Nola Edwards. Second row: Coach Doris Black, Kyle Glenn, Connie McElroy, JoElla Thompson, Angela Taylor, managers Cheryl Trammell and Jeanettte Robinson. Third row: Cheryl Lautt, Jewell Davis, and Tamara Hurt. Photograph courtesy of Robert Logan, Logan Studios.

St. Paul Church of God in Christ was founded in 1972. Shown are members of its Sunshine Band. Those identified are, front row: (1) Antony Ivery, and (4) Diannia Miller. Second row: (1) Daisha Jones, (4) Garry Miller, and (5) Danny Miller. Other churches organized during this decade include Mt. Gilead, Revelation, St. Timothy, and Zebulun Missionary Baptist; Freedom Faith, Freedom Hill, Harvest Grove, and Progressive Baptist. Courtesy of Reverend Earl Blake.

(Right) After winning the 400-meter high hurdles in the 1976 Olympics, Fairview High School/Morehouse College graduate Edwin Moses received the key to the city from Mayor James H. McGee. Moses won 107 straight races from 1977 to 1987, along with a second gold medal in 1984, and a bronze medal in 1988. The United States boycott of the 1980 Olympics kept him from winning a third gold medal. Moses received a master's degree in business administration from Pepperdine University in 1994. Lucinda Adams, a gold medal winner in the 1960 Olympics, was also honored in this ceremony at Courthouse Square. Adams now serves as the supervisor of health, physical education, and driver's education for the Dayton Public Schools. Courtesy of James H. McGee.

(Above) The Ohio Players were the first of the nine local bands to receive a national recording contract during the 1970s. The members were, seated: Clarence Satchall. Second row: Robert Jones, Billie Beck, Marvin Pierce, James Williams, Ralph Middlebrook, and Clarence Willis. Third row: Leroy Bonner and Marshall Jones. The personnel have changed—Ronnie Diamond Hoard served as lead singer on the 1983 album Graduate*—but the Ohio Players continue to tour in the United States and abroad. Courtesy of the* Dayton Daily News.

(Above) The Troutman brothers—Rufus Jr. and Lester (seated) Larry, Roger, and Zapp (standing)—are continuing Dayton's tradition of nationally recognized excellence in music and in business. In 1981 they added the Troutman Construction Company to Troutman Enterprises, which they had established two years earlier to produce and promote Larry, Lester, Roger, and Zapp's music. In November 1993, Zapp and Roger All the Greatest Hits *debuted in the Top Ten of* Billboard's *R & B chart, and in the Top Forty of the pop chart. The Troutmans, who have a commitment to give something back to the community, use their construction company to develop and rehabilitate affordable housing for inner city residents. (Buckins, "Legacy") Courtesy of Troutman Enterprises.*

The expressions on the faces of City Manager Richard Helwig (left), Police Chief Tyree Broomfield (right), and the citizens in the background reflect the tension between the city and the black community during the 1980s. About three hundred citizens rallied at City Hall on September 21, 1987, to protest the chief's decision to fire Majors Edward Long and Phyllis McDonald, a decision they felt was forced upon him by the City Manager and the Fraternal Order of Police. At the rally, Chief Broomfield announced that the majors would keep their jobs. That announcement caused Broomfield to lose city commission support and led to reports that he would be forced out of office. On December 5, 1987, Broomfield resigned. A Waugh Photo, courtesy of the Dayton Daily News.

WDAO 1210 AM

The Real Rhythm of the City

In 1985 WDAO FM was sold to a corporation from Maryland and became an AM station, with Jim Johnson (pictured) as station manager. Johnson served in that role until 1988, when local African Americans formed Johnson Communications, Incorporated, and purchased WDAO, Dayton's first black-owned radio station. At that time "The real rhythm of the city" motif was added to the original logo. Under the leadership of president and general manager Johnson, WDAO continues to be a powerful influence in the Greater Dayton area through its programming, its involvement in community activities, and its newspaper, The Soul/phisticator. *Courtesy of Jim Johnson.*

In 1987 Dr. Sarah Harris, Director of Community Programs at Dayton Power and Light, was appointed Montgomery County Treasurer. She was responsible for managing a budget of $500 million. A year later, she was elected to that position. In the 1990s, Dr. Harris continues to serve the community. In 1991 she became the first African American County Commissioner; in 1993 she became regional director of the Dayton office of the National Conference, formerly known as the National Conference of Christians and Jews. Courtesy of Dr. Sarah Harris.

The 1990s

As Dayton prepares to move into the twenty-first century, African Americans will, like those who preceded them, contribute to all aspects of the community. The people in these thirteen photographs symbolize the efforts of many others, whose names are often unknown.

Clemette Haskins and Oliver Purnell are the first African American head basketball coaches at the University of Dayton. They began to work in the community before the basketball season opened. They served as honorary co-chairs for the American Cancer Society's Cramm'n and Slamm'n 3 on 3 Basketball Tournament in August 1994. Photograph by Larry Burgess, courtesy of University of Dayton Public Relations.

In the area of business and work, Warren Wise, CEO of Wise Construction Company, provides an excellent example of entrepreneurship. Wise started his company in 1983. By 1993, when he was selected as Miami Valley's Entrepreneur of the Year in the area of construction, he had sales of $12.8 million and sixty-six employees. Courtesy of the Wise Construction Company.

In the area of the arts, Jeraldyne Blunden, founder of the Dayton Contemporary Dance Company (DCDC), continues to train new dancers and to provide dazzling entertainment for Daytonians and for people throughout the United States and abroad. A Dayton Daily News *photograph, courtesy of the Dayton Contemporary Dance Company.*

(Above) *In the area of athletics, Roth High School graduate Keith Byars (left), who plays for the Miami Dolphins, and Belmont High School graduate Martin Bayless (right), who plays for the Washington Redskins, are shown at the 1993 Byars-Bayless Football Camp. They established Dayton's first football camp in 1987 to give something back to the community. The camp is free, and teaches young people about football and about strengthening their life skills. Up to thirty professional football players volunteer each summer. Byars and Bayless challenge other Daytonians to serve as positive role models for tomorrow's leaders. Courtesy of the Byars-Bayless Football Camp.*

(Left) Businessman Bob Ross began his rise to ownership of the seven-acre Bob Ross Buick, Inc., complex in Centerville in 1962, when he sold his first car for Shannon Buick in Dayton. Seventeen years later he purchased the Buick dealership and also became the only African American Mercedes Benz dealer in North America. Today he is the operator of one of the Miami Valley's largest service, parts and body shop functions. (Whalen, "Trail Blazer") Courtesy of The Whalen Group.

In 1994, the National Association of Broadcasters honored WROU-FM as the Urban Station of the Year. Shown are, front row: Maria Mann, Sales Assistant; Jeanine Porter, Traffic Coordinator; Donita Montgomery, Promotions Coordinator; Ro Nita Hawes-Saunders, President/General Manager; Rosia Parker, Executive Assistant; Phil Cleveland, Air Personality; and Melanie Babb, Local Sales Manager. Middle row: Bob Summers, Air Personality; Oveda Brown, Account Executive; Norma King, Business Manager; and Le'Andrea Williams, News Reporter. Back row: Jannetta Warren, Receptionist/Secretary; Tony Marcel, Air Personality; Jay Lewis, Part-time Air Personality; Doug Davis, Part-time Air Personality/ Copywriter; Fred Jackson, Account Executive; George Turner, Account Executive; Linda Davis, General Sales Manager; Christian Meinhardt, Account Executive. Courtesy of Hawes-Saunders Broadcast Properties, Inc.

In the area of politics and human rights, Dayton will continue to benefit from the leadership of African Americans at both the local and state levels. Recently elected City Commissioner Dean Lovelace brings to his role valuable experience as a community leader. His work with neighborhoods began in the 1970s when he was active with the Model Cities Program. Later, Dean helped raise funds for community-based initiatives such as the Edgemont Solar Gardens, where he is shown (left) during a Citywide Conference Tour. Courtesy of Dean Lovelace.

Rhine McLin, a former teacher and a businesswoman, began representing the 38th District in the Ohio House in 1989, when she succeeded her father C. J. McLin Jr. Elected to that seat in 1990 and 1992, McLin served on the Finance and Appropriations, and Correctional Institution Inspection Committees, and was vice-chair of the State Government Committee. In 1994 McLin's successful campaign for election to the Fifth Ohio State Senate seat made her the first African American woman in Ohio's upper house. Photograph by Newman Townsend Jr.

In 1991 Idotha "Bootsie" Neal became the first African American woman elected to the Dayton City Commission. "Bootsie" also serves as Assistant Director of Central State University West. She is an active member of many organizations, including the Dayton Alumnae Chapter, Delta Sigma Theta Sorority, Inc., Mt. Enon Baptist Church, the National Council of Negro Women, and the Private Industry Council. Courtesy of Idotha "Bootsie" Neal.

Tom Roberts has represented the Thirty-ninth District in the Ohio House since 1985. He chairs the Committee on Energy and Environment, and serves on several committees, including Aging and Housing, and Children and Youth. Representative Roberts serves on the board of the Black Elected Democrats of Ohio (BEDO), the University of Dayton, and several other organizations. His awards include the Men and Women of Courage Award for Community Outreach. Courtesy of Representative Tom Roberts.

(Left) In Zanesville, Ohio, Mr. and Mrs. Harley Flack, a janitor and a teacher, set high expectations for their children. In 1994 their son, Dr. Harley Flack, was inaugurated as the first African American president of Wright State University. Dr. Flack, who is also a musician, is working to bring the university family and the metropolitan community together. Courtesy of Wright State University.

(Below) One of Dayton's new organizations, Tau Lambda Omega Chapter of Alpha Kappa Alpha Sorority, Inc., began in 1991 as Sisters in Service and was chartered in April 1992. Its projects include Young Sisters Only (YSO). The charter members are, seated: Rhonda Hutchins, Marion Sweeney, Carletta Railey-Worthy, D. Jean Worth, Alma Ivey Clarke, Lynette Heard, Cheryl Grimes, Juanita Jordan, and Patricia Meadows. Standing: Brenda Marone, Lisa Adams, Beverly Jenkins, Brenda Myers, Wanetta Judy Wilson, Angela Durr, Brenda Blane, Lillian Johnson, Crystal Harris, Lisa Taylor, Alice McCollum, and Anita Curry-Jackson. Courtesy of Alma Ivey Clarke.

In the area of religion, Dr. Daryl Ward, pastor of Omega Missionary Baptist Church, also serves as the first African American president of United Theological Seminary. Youth Explosion, which is open to all youths from two to twenty, is one of the many programs he has instituted. These Youth Explosion members stand with Dr. Ward (center) and leader Ricky Smith at Roth Middle School, where they hold services each fourth Sunday. They also engage in community work. These young people possess the same spirit of determination and unity that led Dunbar to write, "O'er all that holds us we shall triumph yet." (Frederick Douglass) With that spirit, they and other young African Americans will be able to meet the challenges of today and tomorrow, and to continue enjoying and enhancing Dayton's African American heritage. Courtesy of Theresa Buycks.

1790

1795
After the Battle of Fallen Timbers (1794), ninety Native Americans signed the Treaty of Greenville, which opened the Miami Valley for settlement by European Americans

1795
Generals Jonathon Dayton, Arthur St. Clair, and James Wilkinson, and Colonel Israel Ludlow purchased land at the junction of the Mad and Miami Rivers. Daniel Cooper laid out the town of Dayton.

1796
The first white settlers arrived in Dayton.

1798
The first reference to a black man was "William Maxwell and his negro" in Dayton Township tax records.

1800-1869

1802
The first African American woman of record was "a colored girl" Daniel Cooper brought to Dayton to be a servant to his family.

1827
Black men working on the canal lived in "Africa," a settlement in Seely's Basin in East Dayton.

1830s
Joe and Nettie Piner began operating an Underground Railroad station.

1839
Local abolitionists formed an antislavery society with Luther Bruen as president.

1841
A proslavery mob attacked black Daytonians living in the area of Fifth, Wayne, and Eagle Streets. One black man killed the leader of the mob.

1850
The basement of First Wesleyan Methodist Church became Dayton's first public school for black children.

1863
Dayton's first Emancipation Day celebration of record was held at First Wesleyan Methodist Church.

1863–65
Forty-six black Daytonians served in the Union Army.

1870-1889

1871
Harriet Wade Boone opened her first beauty salon.

1872
Paul Laurence Dunbar was born.

1881
Warner A. Jackson, Dayton's first licensed black dentist, opened his office.

1889
Dr. William Burns, Dayton's first licensed black doctor, opened his office.

1890
Paul Laurence edited Dayton's first black newspaper, the *Dayton Tattler.* It was printed by Orville and Wilbur Wright.

1892
Dunbar published *Oak and Ivy.*

1897
William Jenkins became Dayton's first black police officer.

1898
Rutherford Moody was one of the black Daytonians who served in the Spanish-American War.

1900-1919

1905
Jacob McFarlane became the first Exalted Ruler of the Waldorf Lodge of the Improved Benevolent Protective Order of the Elks.

1906
Paul Laurence Dunbar died.

Hazey P. Loritts opened Dayton's first black-owned funeral parlor.

1913
Seventy-nine people died in the flood.

John Rives began publishing the *Dayton Forum.*

1915
The Dayton NAACP was formally organized.

1918
The men in Company C, Ninth Battalion, Ohio National Guard, were on the front line for 108 consecutive days.

1920-1939

1920
LeRoy Cox, Dayton's first licensed black pharmacist, opened his drugstore at 842 West Fifth Street.

1922
Dora Rice became Dayton's first black policewoman.

1923
Roosevelt High School opened.

1927
The Classic Theatre opened.

1928
The first public program was held in the Fifth Street YMCA.

1932
Mabel Evens became the first black woman on the Dayton YWCA's Board of Directors.

1933
Dunbar Junior High School opened.

1936
Dave Albritton won the silver medal in the Olympics.

1937
Bernice Johnigan opened Dayton's first Negro beauty school.

1938
The Dunbar House was dedicated as a state memorial.

(Background photo) The back of Linden Recreation Center, Looking north along Horace Avenue. Courtesy of Linden Center.

Local Time Line

1940-1949

1940
The first draft board included Wade Buydden, Hazey P. Loritts, and Roger Prear.

1941
War news ("Negro Air Squadron To Be Trained in Dayton") dominated *Dayton Forum* headlines.

After a campaign by the Dayton NAACP, downtown theaters were opened to "colored people."

Historian J. A. Rogers spoke at the Emancipation Day celebration.

1942
The eighty-seventh annual session of the Amarantha Grand Chapter of the Order of Eastern Star was held in Dayton.

Charity Adams (Earley) became the first Negro commissioned by the WACS.

Mac Ross was among the first five Tuskegee Airmen.

1943
Ads for war bonds and pleas to turn in scrap rubber, paper, and waste kitchen fat were common.

1947
The Dayton Urban League was organized.

Mark Mayo opened the country's first black-owned skating rink.

1948
Donald Ellis became Dayton's first black firefighter.

1950-1959

1950
Fred Bowers became the first black person from Montgomery County elected to the state legislature.

Charles Francis began publishing the *Dayton Citizen.*

Pressure from the NAACP forced downtown restaurant owners to serve black people.

1952
Dr. J. Welby Broaddus became the first black member of the Dayton Board of Education.

1955
W. S. McIntosh organized the Westside Citizens Council, and began conducting demonstrations to force local institutions to end discriminatory practices.

1960-1969

1961
Don Crawford became Dayton's first black city commissioner.

1965
Joseph Saunders began publishing the *Dayton Express.*

Jesse Gooding, president of the Dayton NAACP, led a campaign to force the federal government to end discrimination in employment and job classification. One result was the establishment of a full-time Equal Employment Office at Wright-Patterson Air Force Base.

1966–70s
West Dayton felt the brunt of civil unrest. The Ohio National Guard was called out in 1966 during the first of three "riots." Two of the "riots" were provoked by violence (including the killing of businessman Robert Barbee) by the Dayton police.

1966
C. J. McLin Jr. was elected to the Ohio House of Representatives for the first of eleven terms.

1968
Lawrence Nelson began publishing the *Ghetto News.*

1970-1979

1970
James H. McGee became Dayton's first black mayor.

1972
The NAACP brought suit against the Dayton School Board, charging it with having created a deliberate pattern of segregation.

Ernie Bickerstaff began publishing the *Dayton Black Press.*

1974
The first classes of policewomen who worked as police officers included African Americans Barbara Evans and Jaruth Jefferson.

1975
Desegregation expert Dr. Charles Glatt was murdered.

1976
Court-ordered busing for desegregation began.

The Black Police Officers Association brought suit to force the city to integrate the police force. Only ten percent of the force was black, in a city with a forth percent black population.

1978
Harvey Simmons began publishing the *Jet Stone News.*

1980-1994

1982
The first Dayton Black Cultural Festival was held.

1983
Tyree Broomfield became Dayton's first black police chief.

1984
Richard Clay Dixon became Dayton's second black mayor.

1991
Dr. Sarah Harris became the first African American Montgomery County Commissioner.

Idotha "Bootsie" Neal became the first African American woman on the Dayton City Commission.

1992
The Southern Christian Leadership Conference held its national conference in Dayton.

1993
The Lakeview Palladium, a popular site for both local events and performances by such national artists as Jackie Wilson, was closed and razed to make way for the extension of U.S. 35.

1994
The National Association of Broadcasters named WROU-FM Urban Station of the Year.

"African American Firsts" included Dr. Harley Flack (president of Wright State University), Clemette Haskins and Oliver Purnell (head basketball coaches at the University of Dayton), and Rhine McLin (woman in the Ohio Senate).

1700s

1749–50
French and English struggle to wrest control of the Ohio Valley from Native Americans began.

1776–81
American Revolution.

1787
Northwest Ordinance; U. S. Constitution.

1800s

1808
Slave trade outlawed.

1850
Fugitive Slave Law.

1857
Dred Scott Case.

1861–65
Civil War.

1865–76
Reconstruction.

1895
Booker T. Washington's Atlanta Exposition Speech.

1896
Plessy v. Ferguson.

1900-1919

1905–09
Niagara Movement/ NAACP.

1914–18
World War I.

1920-1929

1921
Harlem Renaissance began.

1929–41
Great Depression.

1930-1949

1939–45
World War II.

(Background photo) The congregation of Bethel Baptist Church at Summit and Home Avenue welcomes servicemen during World War II. Photograph by Norman Stroud.

National Time Line

1950–1959

1950–52
Korean War.

1954
Brown v. Board of Education of Topeka, Kansas.

1955
Montgomery bus boycott began.

1960–1969

1963
March on Washington.

Assassination of President Kennedy.

1964
Civil Rights Bill.

Race riots began in Harlem and other cities.

1965
Assassination of Malcolm X.

Voting Rights Bill.

1966
Dr. King's denunciation of the Vietnam War.

1968
Assassination of Dr. Martin Luther King Jr.

Ten African Americans elected to Congress.

1970–1979

1971
Race riots, shootouts with police continue.

1972
Ohio passes legislation to charter a national Afro-American museum at Wilberforce, Ohio.

Black unemployment worst since the Great Depression.

1973
Thomas Bradley (Los Angeles) became the first black mayor of a large city.

1980–1989

1980
Race riots continued in Miami, Florida, and other cities.

1986
The first Martin Luther King Jr. National Holiday.

1988
The National Afro-American Museum and Cultural Center opens at Wilberforce, Ohio.

1990

1990
Nelson Mandela's tour of the United States.

Anderson, Trezzvant. *Come Out Fighting: The Epic Tale of the 761st Tank Battalion, 1942–1945.* North Carolina: Trezzvant Anderson, 1946.

Austin, Charles. *History of Black People in Dayton and Montgomery County, November, 1807–July, 1887.* Dayton: Charles Austin, 1987.

Bennett, Lerone. *Before the Mayflower: A History of Black America.* Chicago: Johnson Publishing Company, Inc, 1987.

Bernstein, Mark. "In Search of the Well-Known Colored Ball Player," *Ohio Magazine,* April, 1988, pp. 69–70, 112.

Buckins, Sheryl. "The Legacy of the Troutmans…Alive and Well in the 90's." *The Dayton Weekly News,* December 15–22, 1994, p. 15.

Butterfield, Fox. *The Vietnam War: An Almanac.* New York: World Almanac Publishers, Inc., 1985.

Daley, Dave and Rosemary Harty. "Commission Support for Broomfield Ebbs," *Dayton Daily News/The Journal Herald,* September 23, 1987, p. 1.

Davis, Lenwood. "Nineteenth Century Blacks in Ohio: An Historical View," in *Blacks in Ohio, History,* Rubin, ed., Columbus: Ohio Historical Society, 1976, pp. 4-6.

Dayton Urban League. "Pioneers," 1957.

Drury, A. W. *A History of the City of Dayton and Montgomery County, Ohio.* Dayton: S. J. Clarke Publishers, 1909.

Edgar, John. *Pioneer Life in Dayton and Vicinity, 1796–1840.* Dayton: United Brethren Publishing Company, 1896.

Fennessy, Edmund. *An Evaluation of the Dayton Police Department Decentralization and Reorientation Project.* Virginia: PRC Public Management Services, Inc., n.d.

Harris, Marianna. Interviews. September–October, 1994.

Health and Welfare Planning Council of the Dayton Area. *West Dayton Area Profile.* Dayton, 1996.

Jackson, Melody. "Ohio's Mayo Family," *Mainstream America,* February, 1983, pp. 4–6.

Johnson, Charlest. *The Story of One Hundred Years 1842–1942 of the First Wesleyan Methodist Church at Dayton, Ohio.* Dayton, 1942.

Koren, Henry, C. S. Sp. *The Serpent and the Dove: A History of the Congregation of the Holy Ghost in the United States 1745–1984.* Pittsburgh: Spiritus Press, 1985.

Lipper, Hal. "Sound of Dayton," *Dayton Daily News,* March 30, 1988, p. 1-D.

Luckey, Carolyn. *Dunbar and Dayton.* Columbus: Ohio Historical Society, n.d.

Marcano, Ray. "Vietnam Memorial Gets Emotional Dedication," *The Journal Herald,* May 27, 1986, p. 1.

McPherson, Rosamond. *History of the Young Men's Christian Association of Dayton, Ohio 1858–1953.* New York: Association Press, 1953.

BIBLIOGRAPHY

ßMitchell, Fred. *An Architectural and Historical Investigation of the Mound-Horace Area, Dayton, Ohio.* Cincinnati: Historic Preservation Associates, 1993.

Montgomery County Historical Society. *Going to the Source.* Montgomery County Historical Society, n.d.

Montgomery County Recorder's Office. *Record of Deeds Book B,* 1806.

Montgomery County Recorder's Office. *Register of Black and Mulatto Persons for Logan, Greene, Miami, and Montgomery Counties, 1804–1856.*

Newsome, Effie Lee. "Humanitarian at Work," *Jetstone News,* April 2, 1978, pp. 1–2.

Rice, Robert. "Blacks Started Arriving in Dayton in 1798," *Dayton Daily News,* July 4, 1976, p. 4-HH.

Scarborough, Dr. William. "Address at the Unveiling of the Monument to Dunbar, Dayton, Ohio, June 26, 1909," in *Paul Laurence Dunbar.* University Microfilm, n.d.

Schwind, Ida and Ruth Detrick. *One Hundred Years: The Story of the Young Women's Christian Association of Dayton, Ohio, 1870–1970.* Dayton: The Otterbein Press, 1969.

Shelton, William. "Springfield," *Top Magazine,* December, 1960, p. 19.

Steele, Robert and others. *History of Dayton, Ohio.* Dayton: United Brethren Publishing Company, 1899.

U. S. Census. Washington: Government Printing Office, 1820–1990.

Wesley, Charles. *The History of the Prince Hall Grand Lodge of the State of Ohio 1849–1960: An Epoch in American Fraternalism.* Wilberforce: Central State University Press, 1961.

Whalen, Joseph. "Trail Blazer: Bob Ross." Dayton: The Whalen Group, 1994.

Wheeler, Joseph. *History of the Wesleyan Methodist Church and Sunday School from 1842 to 1914.* Dayton: 1914.

White, Luther and others, eds. *Dunbar 50th Anniversary Yearbook.* Dayton: Josten's, 1984.

Williams Dayton City Directories. Cincinnati: Williams Directory Company, 1862–1960.

Newspapers and Newsletters

CityFolk Jazz News
Dayton Citizen
Dayton Daily News
Dayton Forum
Dayton Journal Herald
Express
Jetstone News
Ohio Sentinel

Repositories

Dayton Daily News
Dayton and Montgomery County Public Library
Local church histories
Montgomery County Historical Society
Montgomery County Records Center and Archives
National Afro-American Museum and Cultural Center
Ohio Historical Society
Wright State University, Paul Laurence Dunbar Library Archives

INDEX

Margaret E. Peters

Daytonian Margaret E. Peters graduated from Roosevelt High School in 1954, and earned her B.S., M.A., and Supervisor's Certificate at the University of Dayton.

A teacher for thirty years, she served as Black History Resource Teacher for the Dayton City Schools, and taught African American history at the high school level and at Sinclair Community College. Margaret is a member of the Executive Council of the Association for the Study of Afro-American Life and History (ASALH) and is president of the Dayton ASALH.

Her writings include *The Ebony Book of Black Achievement*, (Johnson Publishers, 1970); "Blacks in Ohio History," (co-author with her brother Wendell) in *Ohio Almanac 1980;* "Goin' Up Yonder," in *Miami Valley History: A Journal of the Montgomery County Historical Society,* May, 1989; and "In Celebration of Black History," *Dayton Daily News,* January, 1992. She also writes a weekly black history column, "From the Root," for the *Dayton Weekly News.*

Miss Peters gives presentations on black history, serves as the church school superintendent at Zion Baptist Church, and is a member of many community groups, including the Southern Christian Leadership Conference. Her honors include the Ohio Martin Luther King Jr. Holiday Commission's Award in Education, the National Council of Negro Women's Excellence in Teaching Award for the Midwestern Region, and the National Education Association's Dr. Carter G. Woodson Award. Photograph by Don Black.

CAMPAIGN
FIFTH
$850,000
MAY
FOR THE MEN